The GREAT COCKCROW Railway

By Jeremy Clarke

This work is respectfully dedicated to the memory of the late AB MacLeod, friend and professional railwayman, and a profound influence on the development of the GCR.

IAN ALLAN Publishing

CONTENTS

First published 1995

ISBN 0 7110 2421 9

Published by Ian Allan Publishing

an imprint of Ian Allan Ltd, Terminal House, Station Approach, Shepperton, Surrey TW17 8AS.
Printed by Ian Allan Printing Ltd, Coombelands House, Coombelands Lane, Addlestone, Weybridge, Surrey KT15 1HY.

INTRODUCTION

Eureka, the symbol of the GCR (*above*) at Greywood driven by owner John Samuel, and (*Below*) some 35 years later driven by her new owner Ian Allan at Chertsey in 1991.

This book is published to celebrate the 25th Anniversary of the 7¼″ gauge Great Cockcrow Railway's opening to the public in May 1969.

The GCR emanated from the pioneering Greywood Central Railway whose growth is also traced. Since the metamorphosis, the GCR has developed into one of the foremost Railways of its type in Europe. With some 2.4km (1½ miles) of track, it is fully-signalled and track-circuited, and is operated strictly in accordance with prototype practice. Its volunteer staff numbers some 50 or so people from all walks of life and includes a fair sprinkling of professional railwaymen.

Operating for 3½ hours on summer Sunday afternoons between May and October, the GCR carries, on average, around 650 passengers per session, or roundly 16,000 in a season.

Many visitors come regularly. Others, including locals unaware of this attraction on their doorstep, express both surprise and delight at finding the Railway, which still retains a low public profile. Yet overseas enthusiasts, from as far away as the Antipodes, who specifically seek out the line, are not uncommon. Very few people leave unimpressed including, it may be said, serving members of the Railway Inspectorate.

This book will, I hope, provide an insight into the Railway's attraction for staff and visitors alike, prove interesting and informative to those who know the line and whet the appetites of those who do not.

ACKNOWLEDGEMENTS

I am very grateful to many GCR colleagues for their help in compiling material for this book, in particular:

Chris Bishop, John Butt, Patrick Egan, Howard Guess, Tony Howker, Jamie Lester, Roger Sills, Phillip Simpson, Richard Stokes and Alan Williams, and Mick Witt who took most of the motive power photographs. Geoffrey Kichenside and my long-time office colleague and friend, Howard Mills, also helped with photographic facilities.

My thanks go to Cynthia Cockle and Angela Brookes for their word-processing expertise and to my wife Karen who, along with the partners of other staff members, has resigned herself to being a 'railway widow' for many Sundays in the year.

And finally, my thanks to Ian Allan, without whom the GCR would not exist.

JC

BEGINNINGS: The Greywood Central Railway

It is an inescapable fact that the Great Cockcrow Railway had its beginnings very firmly anchored in the Greywood Central.

Though much of the original remained following the metamorphosis — track, motive power, rolling stock, signalling equipment, even most of the staff — very different operational emphases and financial environments gave rise to quite individual concerns. Comparisons cannot be drawn. The two railways excel in their own ways. So comparisons become invidious.

Like many a successful enterprise, the Greywood Central began in a very modest way. The period of extreme post-war austerity was not a promising one in which to start such an undertaking, but John Samuel possessed an entrepreneurial spirit that had built up a thriving construction and engineering business.

In the garden of 'Greywood', his home on the Burwood Park Estate at Walton-on-Thames, Samuel had at his disposal an area of almost one acre shaped like the letter 'b'. He put in the first section of line in 1946 for a distance of almost 100 yards along the stem of the 'b' — the western boundary of the site — and through a tunnel beside the house to a two-road terminus in the front garden called Greywood North.

The track consisted of steel bar or angle, but in anticipation of extension Samuel commissioned a more prototypical design in duraluminium from Denis Baglow, who produced 'Fenlow' track at his Weybridge works in 1949; it was first used at Greywood that same year. This initial extension took the form of a large-radius return loop at the South end of the garden which almost tripled the length of run. It also included another of several major engineering works undertaken as the railway

expanded, a fine three-arch brick viaduct taking the line across a pond, 'The Mere'. These works were comparatively small beer to an engineer of Samuel's experience but he lost no opportunity to add to them as the railway grew and they became a characteristic and sometimes spectacular feature of the line.

The next stage, completed in 1951, involved a lengthening of the loop by turning in on itself twice. On its first circuit the line skirted The Mere on a rising gradient to reach a new high point, 'Greymoor Summit', on the northern side of the water. And on the second it ran downgrade through a cutting into the 20 yard-long 'Calgary Tunnel' to bring the track from the centre of the layout to the outside again. A passing place was later incorporated into the outer loop's western end; platforms were provided there, the station being called Mount Hoyt.

A trestle bridge formed another feature of this line. It had to be made easily removable for it crossed the garden path by which the local coal merchant's lorry obtained access to Broad Oak depot. The viaduct built over the eastern half of the original return loop acquired the title 'Christmas Bridge', giving an obvious clue to the time of its construction.

At about this time, Broad Oak depot, built to replace the small storage shed in the front garden, began a period of expansion and development to accommodate an increasing selection of locomotives and rolling stock.

Further development of the track began two years later. Traffic levels had grown so much, despite the house being situated on a private estate, that there was often acute pressure on the small Greywood North terminus. At busy times, the simple track layout there did not have sufficient capacity to cater for the traffic offering. To solve matters, a completely new station, named Jacksonville, was built on a loop at the southern end of the original line from Greywood North. But as part of

Below: Broad Oak depot around 1960 with freelance 'Pacific' *Eureka* passing with an Up train. On shed are NER 'R1' Class 4-4-0, a Stirling 'Single', GCR 'Immingham' Class 4-6-0 and GWR 'Hall' Class 4-6-0 No.7915, *'Mere Hall'* over which John Samuel is bending. The second 'Immingham', on the turntable, is being prepared for service by Phillip Simpson, who is still with the GCR having served as both its General Manager and Mechanical Engineer.

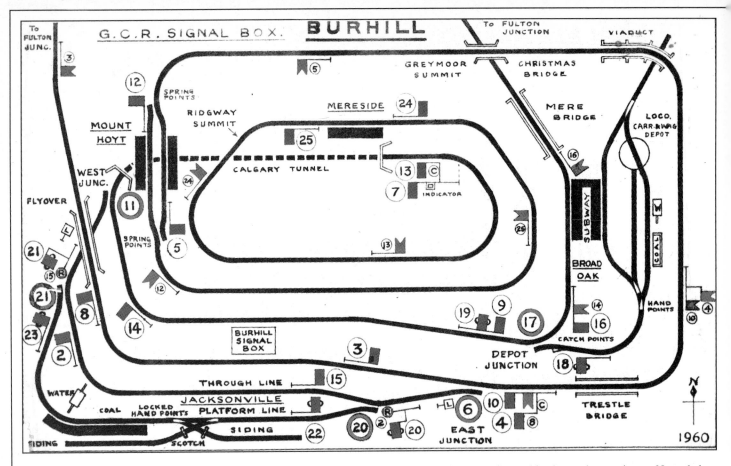

the solution involved relaxing the rigid operating structure imposed by the 'out-and-back' layout which Greywood had been up to that time, a further development wholly changed the character of operations.

The line from Greywood North was slewed over at its southern end and raised on a new embankment to a viaduct and then taken on another new embankment to rejoin its original path in the South-eastern corner of the garden at East Junction, where the line from Jacksonville converged.

West Junction, almost in the western portal of Calgary Tunnel, came into being as the result of construction of a short spur, passing beneath the new Greywood North line viaduct, from the innermost of the coiled extensions to the western end of the loops in Jacksonville station.

These changes, completed in 1953, allowed a continuous run to be introduced. They relieved pressure at Greywood North by concentrating the service on Jacksonville, which had been built alongside a driveway through the estate. The line from Greywood North to East Junction became a branch, though in the timetable introduced in 1960 non-stop services were scheduled to run regularly between Greywood North and Broad Oak.

The easternmost section of the original loop assumed a bucolic existence, being served only by a shuttle service originating from and terminating at Broad Oak.

A year later work started on another inner coil to increase the length of run to about ¾ mile; its route over the spur to West Junction required Calgary Tunnel to be lengthened to thirty yards.

After the engineering works the Railway's signalling system was, perhaps, its most striking feature. Single track throughout, except for the passing loops at Mount Hoyt and Jacksonville stations, the line carried an intensive service in both directions. Semaphore signalling predominated though a small colour-light installation governed movements at Greywood North after 1960.

The first signalbox on the Railway had been put in at Fulton Junction — irreverently known to the staff as Chicken House Junction for quite obvious reasons — where the original line divided into the return loop. This box closed in 1960 upon transfer of signalling responsibility at Greywood North to the stationmaster there.

The whole of the main circuit came under the control of Burhill box, situated alongside the line from Greywood North on its approach to East Junction. The concentration of responsibility in this one place meant that operation was efficient and safe provided signals were properly obeyed.

Despite the long lengths of single track no 'single-line' instruments were used. The life of the signalman at Burhill, however, could be extremely

demanding as the postscript to this chapter bears witness. Nevertheless, the Railway enjoyed an enviable safety record reflecting the greatest credit on its operators.

Much of that could be ascribed to the 'esprit-de-corps' that existed among the staff. While Samuel was the driving force, the recruitment and organisation of the people responsible for much of the construction and operation rested with A. B. MacLeod. He was one of the best-known Southern Railway managers of his day and had been introduced to John Samuel by Captain Howey of the Romney, Hythe and Dymchurch Railway. 'Mac's training and experience as a 'man-manager' proved the ideal foil for Samuel's restless energy. This showed quite clearly in the way responsibilities were divided. Samuel retained an autocratic hand in matters of direction and expenditure but departmental officers were appointed for overseeing such areas as motive power, operation, signalling, permanent way, catering, station management and so on. In this way the railway reached a very high pitch of efficiency which peaked upon the introduction of timetable working in 1960. Plans were then well in hand for further expansion but John Samuel's increasing ill-health meant these were not pursued. He took little part in the 1961 season's operations and still less the following year, finally succumbing to his illness on 23 October 1962 at the early age of 47 and not long after succeeding his cousin in the family Baronetcy.

Although not unexpected, his death was still a severe blow and threw the whole future of the Greywood Central Railway into doubt, though fears that the equipment might be immediately disposed of were allayed when Lady Samuel assured the staff that they had at least two more seasons of operation before them.

In a short time, the GCR had become a great example of what a small-gauge railway could be, given the right direction. Many well-known people, both inside and outside the 'railway world' acknowledged it as superior to anything similar and visited it regularly. Among them, for example, were such figures as J. N. Maskelyne, an authority on all things steam, Terence Cuneo, the artist, who kept an engine there, and Walt Disney, who also figured among its 'Vice-Presidents.' In Disney's opinion no line in the USA matched it for completeness though many exceeded it it size: he came at every opportunity. The Railway's total demise was unthinkable.

Several options on the GCR's long-term future presented themselves. The most optimistic one was that a local purchaser could be found to buy the equipment in its entirety and enlist the aid of the existing staff to rebuild the line on a new site and assist thereafter in its operation. Failing that, it was hoped that the Railway could be retained as a single entity elsewhere in the country. The least attractive option meant the break-up

Left: The 1960 track plan of the Greywood Cental Raiway

Right: An 'Immingham' class 4-6-0 approaches Fulton Junction.

Below: Great Central Railway 'Immingham' Class 4-6-0 and a Southern Railway Class 'V' ('Schools') 4-4-0 stand side-by-side at Greywood North in 1958.

Calgary Tunnel under construction (*above*) and completed (*below*)

Left: The Greywood Viaduct.

Below right: The Chairman of Chertsey Urban District Council cuts the tape under Ian Allan's watchful eye to open officially the Great Cockcrow Railway, 14 September 1968. Driver Phillip Simpson tends the fire in 'K5' 2-6-0 No.206 heading the inaugural train.

of the GCR and its sale in 'job-lots', a prospect nobody, including Lady Samuel herself, relished.

As it became clear that 1964 would, indeed, be the last season of operation, the tentative feelers put out to find a sympathetic purchaser for the line were followed up with vigour during the final months of the Railway's life. It was during this time that an approach was made by MacLeod to the publisher Ian Allan. They were already acquainted, having met in the early 1940s when they both worked for the Southern Railway at Waterloo, the one holding a senior management position on the motive power side, the other being a junior member of the Publicity Department. In this capacity, and as a result of answering numerous enquiries on the subject, Ian Allan had suggested the department should produce a booklet listing the principal dimensions of all Southern Railway locomotives. The suggestion was turned down by his superiors and they initially objected to his publishing such a work on his own account. But the first edition of the *ABC of Southern Railway Locomotives* made its appearance in 1942, gaining the approval of the SR's Chairman, and sold out its 2,000 1/- (5p) copies in a few days. Such was the demand that an immediate reprint became necessary. Similar works for the other three 'Main Line' railways followed and the foundations of today's Ian Allan Group of companies had been laid.

Ian had visited Greywood on a number of occasions since the mid-50s. He was clearly impressed with the Railway and, equally clearly, the opportunity to acquire the equipment interested him. He had already contemplated constructing a line of his own at some time on farmland purchased some years before only a few miles away at Chertsey. MacLeod's negotiations with him came to a successful conclusion late in 1964, to the corporate relief of the staff whose continued connection with the GCR was assured at the same time. It seemed hard to believe that the most optimistic of the options open to them had, indeed, been taken up.

Preparations for the move began at once though some months were to elapse before any equipment was shifted as a local farmer still rented the new site at the time. Dismantling started in earnest on 4 July 1965 and the last run over the circuit, by a 2-8-2 locomotive on test after refurbishment took place on 15 August before track lifting on a large scale began. The 'R1' was the last engine to be steamed at Greywood, taking a visiting party over the truncated line between Greywood North and Calgary Tunnel on 19 September. The final lengths of track came out on 30 January 1966 and a week later demolition of the pioneering and once proud 'Greywood Central Railway' was complete.

THE BURHILL PRAYER

Good Lord of all poor signalmen, please send me down a sign,
I've two trains in the circuit and Mere Hall's off the line.
Charles is stuck in Jacksonville a'raking of his fire,
And Greymoor Summit's blazing just like a funeral pyre.
Phillip just passed Fulton at sixty miles or more,
(I hope the road to Greywood is clear but I'm not sure).
The tablet's lost, 'eleven' points are up the bloody creek,
The telephone rings all the time but no one comes to speak ...!!
Good Lord of all poor signalmen please guide my clueless hand,
And if I cause an accident, pray 'Mac' will understand.

TRANSITION: *The Move to Chertsey*

The staff had their first close look at the Railway's new home on 20 June 1965.

The prospect that greeted them was, to say the least, unpromising. Too poor for cultivation, the field had been used as a piggery. Parts of it were very boggy and there was a large, muddy pond near the western boundary. Many of the trees had been severely damaged by the pigs stripping the bark, some beyond recovery, and the whole site was a riot of weeds and brambles. There was one bright spot though — size! At around 185m by 80m at extremes and some 1.18 hectares (about 3 acres) overall, the area available came to about three times that in the garden at 'Greywood.' The field generally sloped toward the East with a steep drop across the middle of the site, of almost a metre and a half by the northern boundary reducing to a metre or so at the South side. Though classified as farmland the area was useless for anything save the most basic of farming purposes. Provided the proposed buildings were acceptable to the Local Authority there seemed to be no reason why a change of use should not be permitted.

Tentative plans for the sheds to house locomotives and stock were drawn up on 11 July, three days after senior staff met Ian Allan to discuss proposals for the new layout. Some talk at that meeting centred around a new name for the Railway: 'Greywood Central' was now clearly inappropriate. Several suggestions had been considered before someone pointed out that the nearest landmark, a small knoll called Cockcrow Hill, adjoined the site. 'Great Cockcrow Railway' perpetuated the original 'GCR' initials. It was a good omen.

When the winter frosts had burned off all but the hardiest vegetation, a rough survey was made of the proposed site of the main terminus. This showed a height difference of nearly two metres between West and East ends and that the ground fell away towards the North-East corner. Levelling up promised to be a long job. Although most of it would be done by a bulldozer, tools and equipment would still be needed for much of the work, so two redundant containers to house them were acquired from BR together with a number of old sleepers for a foundation. A small area by the western boundary was cleared, levelled and covered with a layer of shingle to assist drainage before the containers were lowered into place on 16 March 1966. Two weeks later, the terminal site had been accurately surveyed, datum fixed and the required levels pegged out ready for the bulldozer.

This work proved very difficult, for the pegs had to be dug accurately into the higher ground. Along the southern boundary the ground shelved gently for about 55 metres before falling away into the sharp dip. Datum was fixed a little under one metre below the level at the West end to ensure that the track into the main field could be laid on a relatively easy gradient and to provide spoil for an embankment to achieve this across the dip.

The proposed plan for the terminus showed a small turntable in the South-Eastern corner, set above the surrounding ground and approached by a sharply-graded bank, to give access to the loco shed, in which the tracks would be raised above the floor. The platform and carriage shed roads and the engine release line through the station, from which the loco shed access was taken, all fed into a large turntable, of 4.8m diameter, located in the South-western corner of the site.

It was several weeks before the bulldozer could begin work. The subsoil on site is a pebbly, fine-grained clay, as hard as concrete when dry but slimy and unstable when wet, presenting the Civil Engineer with the delicate problem of deciding when it had dried out sufficiently to bear the weight of the machine yet still retained enough moisture to make it workable. In the meantime, the terminus was enclosed in a high, chain-link fence broken only by two sets of double gates, one to give access from the main entrance in Hardwick Lane, the other positioned where the tracks would go out into the main field. Beyond those lower gates floodwater stood several inches deep in places and the pond overflowed, adding its quota to the already sodden ground around it. The ditches adjoining the field were found on inspection to be choked with mud and decaying vegetation preventing the excess water from draining away. Clearance was essential if any progress was to be made in the main field so the more hardy members set to, working throughout March and well into April, standing sometimes thigh-deep in the icy water and often knee-deep in slime, shovelling the stinking mess out on to the banks. Several hundred metres of ditching, up to three or four fields away, had to be cleared in this way until the flow of drainage water was sufficient to scour out the muck. Similar attention was paid to the stream running through the South-Eastern corner of the field for, although the water flowed quite freely along it, a thick layer of debris on the bed raised its level a half-metre or more, restricting its effectiveness in draining the land bordering on to it. Significantly, all this work had little effect on the large pond but as that was not delaying progress on the main station site it was left until the following year.

Left: Eureka is signalled into platform 1 as she arrives at Hardwick Central with an Up train. in 1970.

Right: Coasting down from Piggery Summit at Fork Junction, where the Loop divided, is Class 'S15' 4-6-0 No.837 in 1970.

By early summer, conditions were considered good enough for the terminus to be levelled off, the work being done by a bulldozer-equipped 'Fordson' tractor. Spoil was clawed out of the 'wedge' of high ground in the South-Western corner of the site and pushed into the lower parts toward the North and East, the excess being left on the Eastern boundary. A resurvey followed to ensure none of the pegs had been disturbed and remained accurately set, particular attention being paid to those that had had to be sunk far below the original ground level. This resurvey showed how well the contractor had performed, working to very close tolerances and so considerably reducing the anticipated amount of follow-up work. The survey also accurately fixed the position of the large turntable and, after pegging out, a start was made on excavating its pit to a depth of 40cm below the new ground level.

Work on the terminus occupied much of the summer despite the flying start provided by the Fordson, for the spoil from the turntable pit had to be barrowed the length of it to be added to a dump on the eastern boundary whence the embankment across the drop would be pushed into the main field. Moreover, the wretched stuff dried out, inevitably slowing up the work.

During that season too, scores of lengths of track recovered from Greywood — the grounds there were not finally cleared until mid-February 1967 — were brought in and stacked in a corner of the site to await relaying as the earthworks progressed.

By late-summer the area was level enough for another intensive survey to fix the positions of the tracks from the platforms to the lower gates. These positions were pegged for both course and height before the whole track area was troughed out to a depth of 25-30cms to accept a blanket of 5cm shingle ballast for drainage purposes. This blanket had absorbed several lorry-loads of shingle, barrowed in from a dump by the main gate, before the great day, appropriately 1 January 1967, when the first lengths of track were laid down. A second, parallel road with a crossover to the first, was installed a week later. This work permitted several wagons to be withdrawn from store to run on the line, considerably easing and generally speeding up the task of shifting spoil and ballast.

The start of the new year saw spoil from the terminus site gradually pushed into the main field to form the embankment. There was no question of clearing the ground first. While the smaller undergrowth simply vanished beneath the advancing spoil, a swathe was hacked through the bigger stuff, soon earning the section the nickname 'Polish Corridor.'

As the embankment progressed one track was extended along it from the terminus site to bring spoil as close as possible to the point where tipping was going on.

Although the bank began to settle and compact under the combined influence of men and materials moving along the top, it remained relatively unstable, particularly after rain. So a start was made in mid-April on stripping large areas of the field of its top turf covering to lay along the embankment sides. Topsoil was similarly acquired to aid the bedding-in process of the turf. This work and the grading of the bank up to datum went on throughout the summer until, by the middle of September, the Polish Corridor was ballasted and ready for a double line of rails.

Despite the prolonged efforts on this section, other projects were well in hand. Late in March active steps were taken to drain the pond which, once more, had overflowed during the winter. A ditch runs alongside Hardwick Lane, adjoining the western boundary of the site, and the engineers breached the bank separating it from the pond. This was only partially successful and a more far-reaching course later became necessary. As it was, nearly three months elapsed before the water level had fallen sufficiently to allow the Fordson to be called in again.

A deep cutting was clawed straight through the wooded area between the edge of the pond and the southern end of the scarp so prominent on the North side. Spoil from this cutting went into an embankment through the middle of the pond itself while the mass that remained was piled along the edge of the wood adjoining the North/South drop to form part of the proposed 'Phase 2' of development.

Most of this work was carried out with the reek of smoke hanging around the trees, the result of huge bonfires of evil-smelling rubbish dragged out of the pond or dumped in its vicinity. Clearly the place had been used for years as a repository for unwanted junk!

Clearance of a way through the copse on the segment bounded by the stream was initiated on 18 June 1967. That same day staff were advised of the granting of Planning Permission which, doubtless, lent added impetus to the arms hacking their way through the tangle of birch, hazel and willow saplings.

At the eastern end of the field work was progressing on raising the ground between the end of the Polish Corridor and the stream. Some of the spoil for this shallow embankment came from the ground alongside it and, by the time the work was done and the bank levelled and turfed, a new pond had formed in the excavations.

Meanwhile, the pond at the western end, now split into two of course, was giving trouble again, filled to overflowing by the autumnal rain. The Hardwick Lane ditch coped well with the water on its side of the embankment but the drainage channel in the new cutting through the woods was overwhelmed by high levels in the isolated segment. So, in mid-October, the Fordson was called in again, to take a slice out of the embankment so that a large-diameter pipe could be sunk to reunite the two halves of the pond.

Above: Eureka *climbs away from Everglades Junction anticlockwise around the loop towards Piggery Summit in 1970, passing the Down Home bracket signal.*

At the same time the breach to the Hardwick Lane ditch was deepened but this had the effect, after heavy or prolonged rainfall, of reversing the flow of water from the ditch into the pond. Only by ensuring that the bed of the ditch was kept clean could draining of the pond be guaranteed.

As Christmas approached, the staff could take much satisfaction from the progress made in the two years since Greywood's demise. But second thoughts were being expressed on the proposed arrangements for the engine shed. These had been designed to satisfy the requirements of the motive power staff who preferred to have engines at around waist level when they worked on them, quite apart from the necessity of having to have access beneath them at times. The arrangement of raising the track off the ground had been planned on the reasonable assumption that the water-table was close to the surface of the new ground level. But as it had not been breached when the large turntable pit was dug out, an exploratory borehole was sunk on the proposed site of the loco shed in early January, when the water level could be expected to be near its highest. Contrary to expectations water was not reached until the hole was almost a metre deep, indicating that it would be possible to bring the track in at ground level over inspection pits after all. Despite progress already made on the raised approach to the small turntable and on its site, which was almost complete, this course was adopted. Not only would it provide a more aesthetically pleasing arrangement as a whole but the large turntable was already located in such a position that the additional roads could be taken off it without difficulty.

In the light of these changes the decision was made to reverse the originally planned uses of the two sheds: the carriage shed would house the locos instead, and the engine shed the stock. They would take seven roads between them, three for engines, two having pits inside and outside the building, and four for stock, also providing sufficient accommodation for the goods vehicles. Plans were redrawn on this basis.

In October 1967 the sides of the turntable pit were reinforced with a circular retaining wall, a fine example of the bricklayer's craft. A concrete ring for the supporting track was laid in November while the rest of the floor received the usual shingle drainage blanket.

The table itself is timber-built, two deep baulks cross-braced to gauge with a rail screwed to the head of each one. A centre-mounted timber block, planed to exact width, fits between the baulks and is accurately drilled to take a close-fitting steel tube to contain the pivot. A bearing plate beneath this block transfers the entire weight of the turntable on to a massive ballrace set on the pivot. (The outriggers with flanged wheels running on the supporting rail merely steady the table in movement).

The present turntable replaced the original in 1977. It has slides at each end to ensure proper alignment of the rails with the relevant fixed track and is provided with cantilevered timber walkways.

The new loco shed arrangements required construction of a drainage channel for the inspection pit. This was marked out between the projected position of the pit and the ditch at the Hardwick Lane

boundary and dug early in the New Year. Salt-glazed pipes were laid in the trench before the whole area between the site of the sheds and the turntable was excavated to the usual 25-30cm depth for a shingle drainage bed. Spoil from this work and from the footings of the carriage shed and the signalbox foundations, was taken to be added to the embankment beyond the Polish Corridor or to a dump by the stream. This transportation work was much lightened and speeded-up on 18 February when the first locomotive to run on the line made its appearance on test. The engine was the prototype of a battalion that eventually provided motive power for many commercial lines around the country,. An 0-4-0 chain driven off a 'Petter' 3hp diesel engine, Thunderbolt' was grossly overscale, heavy and noisy but proved capable of hauling any weight the engineers cared to put behind her.

The rapid progress made in the terminus area permitted a delivery of concrete blocks for the sheds and signalbox to be made at the beginning of March: two weeks later the carriage shed walls had reached roof level. By that time too, the concrete floor of the signalbox had been poured, the level frame bolted into place and the walls raised up to track level. (The floor is sunk some 50cm below that). By mid-April 1968 the two buildings were complete and the Signals and Telecommunications staff were busy interlocking the lever frame and setting up the connections to be run in due course to the points and signals.

At about this time a 'gang' was formed to attend exclusively to the monumental task of refurbishing the track. Broken or rotten sleepers were stripped from the track lengths stored on site and replaced from among the thousands of new sleepers which, over the preceding year, had been cut, jig-drilled for track screws and left to soak in a mixture of creosote and used motor oil. The oldest and most worn track, including some of Greywood's earliest 'L' section girder type, was lightly sleepered and earmarked for laying in the carriage shed. The four tracks there were installed and troughed through the drainage ballast to the turntable over a three-week period in May.

When the Civil Engineering staff had finished building the carriage shed and signalbox their attention turned to the problem of bridging the stream. Incentive to complete this and other essential work was provided by the news that 14 September had been fixed as the official 'Opening Day' and much still needed to be done. The width of the stream and the angles at which the line would cross it at the two points selected gave scope for variety in bridging methods. The upstream point is narrow, barely 2.5m across, and bounded by deep, almost vertical banks. By contrast, although no wider at water-level, the downstream crossing had shallower, shelving banks. It was decided to build a girder bridge here and to enclose the stream in a piped culvert at the narrower point.

To allow foundations for the girders to be put in, earth coffer dams were formed and the banks cut back behind these and trenched out below the stream's floor level so that shuttering for the base rafts could be accurately positioned and fitted into place. The rafts were cast on successive weekends at the end of June and the two concrete beams on each raft had been successfully shuttered and poured within the next three weeks, despite time lost through torrential rain. The 15cm (6″) 'RSJ' girders of 4.7 metres span, with the lugs for attaching the handrails already welded in place, were taken out to the site by rail and drawn into position on 28 July. Crossbracing and reinforcing steels between the girders were positioned and braced up before the concrete floor itself was 'floated' across the supporting shuttering and a polythene membrane over two successive weekends early in August. Track was laid across the bridge later that same month when the handrails had been fitted and painted. Like most sections and works on the Railway the bridge soon acquired a name, in this instance being called after the staff member who had designed it and fabricated the steelwork. Indeed, the whole area around it soon became known generically as 'Phillips Bridge.'

The bridge came into regular use immediately for trains of spoil proceeding through The Copse to the new culvert. From 1 September these were steam-hauled, the 'K5' 2-6-0 being the first engine to raise steam on the new GCR. The culvert is formed of three large-diameter pipes laid in the stream bed, spoil being tipped above and around them to fill in the open area between the banks: concrete retaining walls were constructed later. Ballast to fettle the track through The Copse was also brought in by the 'K5' while intensive preparations for the great day went on elsewhere. The signal installation at Hardwick Central was put through its final testing and adjustment: track along the Polish Corridor had some last-minute fettling done: lengths of paling fence for the public 'circulating' area were set in place: coaches, long in store, were cleaned and their bogies greased and adjusted before, on 14 September 1968, 'K5', 'R1' and 'Eureka' raised steam and the Great Cockcrow Railway officially opened its gates for business.

DEVELOPMENT: *The basic layout Complete*

Despite a Mayoral presence at the Opening Ceremony, not even the most enthusiastic or partisan member of staff could claim the day was an unqualified success.

Restrictions on advertising — at the insistence of the Local Authority and a condition of the Planning Consent — allied to heavy rain during the morning limited the number of passengers, although thirty trains were run for the public during the afternoon. Nevertheless, it was a start and the pungent reek of coal smoke, steam and hot oil put new heart into the staff as well as into the engines.

The remainder of 1968 was given over to working on the return loop through 'Pig Pond', the name applied very early on in the Railway's life to the wooded area at the West end of the field as well as to the pond itself. (The new, more euphonious name 'Everglades' had yet to be assimilated and was rarely used during the constructional period nor for some time afterwards.)

Rail access to the Pig Pond area depended on the completion of the shallow embankment West of the stream. As this crosses a marshy patch of ground in was soon dubbed 'The Causeway', equally quickly it became known as 'Chat Moss', for material tipped there vanished almost as fast as it arrived. Further, it proved notoriously unstable, the sides bulging out under any pressure on top of the bank, particularly after rain. It was not until ditches had been dug out alongside it to drain off water into the stream and the turf finally secured a hold after several false

Below: SR 'S15' Class 4-6-0 raises the echoes as she comes off The Causeway on the climb to Piggery Summit in 1980, driven by Chris Bishop, the GCR's current General Manager. The train is made up of 'standard' coaches.

starts, that the bank assumed any degree of permanence. Even in more recent times spoil has had to be added to the sides periodically to replace material lost in the bog, a common, though lesser need with other embankments on the railway. Spoil was brought in by rail of course, motive power being provided by the little diesel-shunter 'Winifred.' Having been in store for over two years, it took some patient tinkering to get her started, but on her first outing on 28 September she moved forty wagon-loads of material away from the Hardwick loco shed pit and worked consistently at this level over the following four weekends.

A survey showed that between Chat Moss and Everglades the Southern half of the loop could surmount the intervening ridge on a reasonable gradient if a cutting was excavated at the highest point, christened immediately and inevitably 'Piggery Summit'. This cutting, less than a metre deep, was dug out by hand, spoil from one side of the summit going down to Pig Pond embankment and the other to Chat Moss. Reasonable weather ensured good progress so that by the end of December, following some very smart work by the track gang, the track was in place from The Copse right through to Everglades.

Three weeks into the New Year the loop had been completed, though ballasting and some drainage work through the deep Pig Pond cutting occupied the rest of January. As part of these works, a new section of track to allow a continuous run was surveyed; experience of Greywood's rigid out-and-back prior to the opening of Jacksonville station ensured that the more flexible arrangement would be perpetuated.

It was planned to build a passing loop and station on this section. The back of the ridge marking the southern boundary of Hardwick Central station had to be cut away to make room for part of the Down platform, the spoil going into the embankment needed across the scarp. Spoil also came from Hardwick itself where excavations of the platforms were being made. Being interspersed with other work the embankment was not completed until early May 1969.

Much of this other work centred on the engine shed. The floor had been cleared and levelled for concreting the previous November but the foundations for the walls were not dug out until March. Screeding the floors of both the shed and the inspection pit occupied four weekends. And as if their appetite for concrete remained unsatisfied, the engineers set up formers and laid the island platform at Hardwick by the end of April. The engine shed building itself was finished in June. Like the adjoining carriage shed it measured 12m by 2.75m internally.

The drain on staff resources however, when the Railway operated on alternate Sundays throughout the 1969 summer, and work on the Spur line between Everglades and Phillips Bridge, combined to defer tracklaying in the shed until the Autumn, although it is convenient to deal with it here.

The tracks spanning the pit are fabricated frames of steel angle, tube and plate, largely welded together for strength and tautness.

The tube is used for the main supports with a plate set across the top, strutted for strength by small section angle sprung off the tube itself. The plate supports the main girders made of large-section angle which, with the flange upright, form the track itself inside the shed. The girders are inverted on the outside section with track bolted to the horizontal upper face.

Holes had been left in the pit floor for the tubular uprights, and when each track section had been set up and was accurately held in position the holes were filled with concrete. As each track is in three lengths there were six such sections to be dealt with, taking a period of seven weeks between November and January to put into place.

The outside pit, 2.7m long, has only one support for each track; the inside one, being 5.8m long, required four supports; the one closest to the sill between the pit's inner and outer sections, provides extra support where the two sections meet by having steel angle sprung off the bottom of the tube and cantilevered on the longitudinal line of the track to additional bearer plates. Work began in February 1970 on tracklaying in the rest of the shed, including the third road, which did not have a pit, and from the pit to join up to the turntable. Once these tracks were in place the brick topping was added to the pit walls and the ballast backfilled up to level, a task completed by the end of the month when the engines, at last, took up residence.

Meanwhile, progress had been made during the Summer of 1969 on the Everglades — Phillips Bridge 'Spur' line and the development of the junction as noted earlier. The 'passing loop' layout in use since the previous September was augmented by a third road laid on the Down side and up the Polish Corridor toward Hardwick. This road was complete and ballasted by 22 July. Two weeks later the track from Hardwick was cut near the top of the bank and slewed over to join up with it, releasing the existing track for incorporation into the Spur. The line from Everglades reached this severed portion in mid-August enabling the new arrangements, together with the associated pointwork at Phillips Bridge, to be brought into use on 7 September when the signalbox there was also commissioned. In this interim phase of development directional use of track at Phillips Bridge was rather unusual. Each single, reversible line on the Polish Corridor could be reached only from one of the two Up Loops, so segregation of Hardwick- and Everglades-bound trains was made at the extreme Down end of the layout by the only point worked from the box. (All other points were sprung). Down trains from both single lines were routed into the centre road, the Down Loop. Though not ideal, this formation had the advantage of keeping conflicting moves to a minimum.

Despite this work the Spur did not come immediately into regular service as the track connections and signalling at Everglades were not completed until the spring of 1970. The Everglades loop over Piggery Summit and through Pig Pond Cutting was controlled in the interim by a temporary ground frame at Fork Junction.

The site for Everglades signalbox had been cleared and the foundations laid the previous November but, with attention focused over the winter on tracklaying in the engine shed, further work was deferred until the New Year.

The edge of the bank upon which the box stands had to be cut back to form a pit to accommodate the interlocking mechanism. Shuttering for the retaining wall at the back of this pit was set up and the concrete poured at the beginning of February. The footings to the rear and side walls of the box itself and the concrete floor were finished towards the end of March. A week later the lever frame had been put into place but further construction was put back until the close season, though the lintel over the operating cables from the frame was cast *in situ* in August.

A further quantity of track arrived at the end of 1969 from the defunct 7¼"/10¼" dual gauge railway at Bassetts Manor, the 'third rail' being stripped from most of the lengths for reuse. Some of this went into the construction of two new points; one was incorporated into the crossover connections at Fork Junction while the other provided access to a siding into the ballast storage area established at Everglades. To complement this facility and to facilitate transhipment of the ballast into wagons for transport, a new siding was taken off the turntable at Hardwick into the passenger circulating area where deliveries were normally received. The ground there was excavated along the course of the siding to bring the rail head down to ground level, and when the steel track had been laid and levelled up concrete was poured into the excavated section. This facility was complete by December 1970. With the imminent proliferation of 10¼" gauge seaside lines built under Ian Allan's auspices, a third-rail had been laid alongside this road and added to the turntable in preparation for the provision of winter storage facilities for some of the commercial rolling stock.

A generator set given on indefinite loan by its owner arrived in the Autumn of 1969. Driven by a water-cooled donkey engine, it produced 750w of current at 240v AC, rectified and stepped-down as required before distribution.

Initially, feeds were provided in the signalboxes for instrument and indication purposes, and in the loco shed where steam-raising was assisted by electrically-driven compressors.

The set was housed in the engine shed and operational for the 1970 season, the exhaust pipe protruding through the adjacent wall. Until the arrival of mains power on site in the mid-seventies, operations were conducted against the background of a monotonous 'put-put-put-put' as the generator thumped its way through the afternoons.

A hosepipe buried in the ground carried a supply of mains water from a tap in a barn, some 60m away across the car park, to a standpipe in the passenger circulating area. This standpipe had been erected during the constructional period but it was clearly inconvenient to ferry water for loco purposes from it to the station when the place was crowded with people. So an alternative supply was set up during the 1970 summer.

This entailed mounting a 400-gallon galvanised iron tank on a plinth alongside the engine shed with the guttering arranged to feed rainwater off the roof into it and thence to water cranes in the station and the loco pit. The most difficult part involved excavating a soakaway for the overflow and trenching out pipe runs in that appalling subsoil. At the same time, more hose was buried in the ballast so the tank could be replenished from the standpipe if the water level ran low. This work was complete by the end of June; a month later the manifold connections were fitted and the system brought into service.

When the Committee members met that autumn, the basic layout was almost compete and preparations were in hand for doubling the track into Hardwick Central and between Phillips Bridge and Fork Junction.

Both these projects involved a slight change in the layout at Phillips Bridge. In preparation for this a point was laid in the Spur where it diverged away from the Hardwick Central line on the Polish Corridor. Once more, the track was severed, and slewed across to join up with the point, while the incipient Down road from Hardwick Central was extended down the bank to join the erstwhile reversible single line to Phillips Bridge. At the far end of Phillips Bridge the lever-worked point became spring controlled; operation was transferred instead to the new point at the Spur divergence which would thereafter segregate Hardwick-bound trains from those to Everglades. The use of the tracks at Phillips Bridge now became more conventional with one Down loop for trains from Hardwick and another for those from Everglades — the centre road of the three — while all Up trains were routed into the single Up Loop. As before the short section of track between the Spur divergence and Phillips Bridge remained bi-directional, but the erstwhile reversible line between Hardwick Central and Phillips Bridge was now for use of Down trains only.

Attention turned at the beginning of January 1971 to the completion of the signal box (now the relay room) at Everglades. Like the building in Hardwick station this is of concrete block construction. The walls were completed by the middle of February and a month later the window frames had been built up and fitted into place. At the time they were unglazed and several years were to elapse before most of the draughts that invaded the building as a result were finally eliminated with the fitting of sliding sashes. A delay in the delivery of suitable timber held up construction of the roof but this was complete by the first week in May and the box was commissioned in time for the opening day of the season later that same month.

Making up three more points to go into the crossovers at Fork Junction began in January and they were laid in place on 7 March. Track to form the new Up line was extended from them across The Causeway: as yet though Bishops Culvert was not wide enough to take it because it had originally been decided to leave doubling through to Phillips Bridge until the following autumn. But the steady increase in traffic during the early summer caused this to be brought forward. Construction of the downstream retaining wall of the culvert for this purpose began in late July. Inner and outer sets of shuttering were erected with steel reinforcing rods positioned between them before the concrete was poured over two successive weekends early in August. A week later, the inner part of the shuttering was removed, the gap backfilled with soil and the site cleared and levelled before the trackbed was dug out and ballasted. By the end of August the Up line track extended through The Copse to the loop at Phillips Bridge, eliminating the point at the extreme Down end there. Services over it began the following weekend.

The siding at Everglades had been laid in early in 1971. Its main purpose, as previously mentioned, was to serve the Railway's ballast storage area and an earth bank was raised to form a retaining wall between this area and the deep Pig Pond cutting which ran parallel and at a lower level to it. To provide a wide enough base for this bank the drainage ditch in the cutting had to be shifted over to the opposite side of the trackbed. Work on both the ditch and the siding complex was finished by late-April and the first ballast consignment to be stored there arrived on 9 May.

Ballast proved to be an underestimated source of expense. The trackbed swallowed more enormous quantities during that close season with seemingly little effect at the time. But as the ballast settled and firmed

during the summer, accidents due to track deficiencies declined sharply, though one of the two articulated carriage sets 'split' a set of points in a serious derailment on 27 June, shearing off its centre bogie and causing considerable damage to the track; fortunately nobody was hurt. All main line points came under close scrutiny the following weekend as a result and were fettled up where necessary. Despite this corrective action derailments continued to occur on the point at the top of the Polish Corridor where The Spur diverged from the Up Main. It had been persistently troublesome since being placed into this position despite constant attention to level and alignment. Drastic surgery was performed on 28 August when the point was completely rebuilt *in situ* with success.

Another persistent problem first showed up in spectacular fashion in July when some parts of the track buckled seriously out of line as the temperature rose during the morning. Fishplates in the vicinity had to be loosened and re-lubricated to release the stresses before services could begin running. The high expansion factor of duralumin is the main cause of the problem which has never been solved with complete satisfaction, though the insertion of expansion joints in the more lengthy stretches of plain track exposed to strong sunlight has certainly eased matters. However, long, sweeping curves still tend to spring outwards despite careful fettling and consistent maintenance of fishplates and bolts. Experience has shown that pegging the curves into place merely transfers the problem elsewhere! The only answer seems to be the judicious use of a club hammer to spread the stress evenly throughout the curve.

Slippages on The Causeway embankment over the winter, due to the blockage and flooding of the drainage ditches alongside it, had to be repaired. Re-turfing the sides of the bank began in March, while the ditches themselves were cleared out and deepened during the spring months. Much other work undertaken then and into the summer was of a cosmetic nature — building up edging along embankments, around point mechanisms and at the front of signal boxes — to prevent the ballast falling away from under the track; painting buildings and creosoting timber structures and clearing and tidying the working area in the compound at Hardwick which at times could be something of an eyesore. By the time the 1971 season drew to the close on 3 October, and despite running a record number of trains on alternate Sundays during the year, the staff had brought about a noticeable improvement to the Railway and its surroundings. They had in prospect too, their first taste of nightime operation at Chertsey. The Shepperton Rotary Club proposed to hold a firework party in the grounds on the first Saturday in November and as an added attraction the Railway was to be open to the public. This provided an ideal opportunity to get rid of some of the more dangerous trees in the Everglades area: over the intervening weekends several were felled and cut up as fuel for the bonfire. The evening proved a great success and was repeated for some years afterwards.

Work began on the morning after that first Bonfire Night on the upstream wall of Bishops Culvert with the outer 'skin' of shuttering being set into place. The inner part and the reinforcing were fitted up a week later, the wall being poured on 21 November. By the end of the month the shuttering had been dismantled and the section backfilled with soil and ballast leaving only the brick capping to be added to the walls. But it never was. Though scheduled for completion on several subsequent occasions it was not a vital job and seemed to get pushed aside whenever anything else more important cropped up. Eventually, in recognition of the inevitable, the reinforcing rods forlornly protruding through the top of each wall were sawn off flush.

The year was finally seen out with the pouring of an additional foundation to the signalbox at Phillips Bridge to provide support for a precast concrete-section shed purchased as a replacement for the timber clapboard structure in use there since the Railway opened. Nobody quite realised then for just how short a period this new building would serve its intended purpose.

Left: Mere Hall departs from a moderately-crowded Hardwick Central on a 'circuit' working in 1984. *Eureka* waits to enter the Headshunt.

Below left: A new Down end Loop-to-Main crossover at Everglades Junction was installed in 1976 in connection with the Branch. The empty ballast wagons await return to Hardwick

Below: A short 'closure' section is still needed to complete the trackwork of the new Down Loop/Down Main crossover at Everglades Junction.

Above: During 1970, train delays were sometimes frequent because of congestion on the single track. The passengers do not appear to mind but the driver of 4-6-2 *Eureka* looks as though he is used to it!

Below: Another 1970 shot; because the route between Phillips Bridge and Hardwick was of single track only right-hand running was used at Phillips Bridge. The line's Class K5 2-6-0 is seen at speed passing the signal box.

Right: Motive power line up at Hardwick Depot, with SR Class S15 4-6-0 No. 837, a visiting Stanier Class 5 4-6-0 No. 4871, LMS 4-6-0 No. 6100 *Royal Scot* and in the background a North Eastern R1 4-4-0 of the type that became LNER D19.

RETHINK: *The Layout revised*

Before the close of the 1971 season it had become ominously clear that the layout was proving difficult to work efficiently. And the realisation that the number of passenger journeys would almost certainly continue to increase gave the Committee much food for thought. Before describing the results of its deliberations, however, it might be prudent to examine the circumstances that led to the adoption of the layout design in the first place.

With the exception of Ian Allan himself and the Railway's General Manager, Geoffrey Kichenside, all the Committee members had come from Greywood. None of them had had any other extensive experience of building or operating railways of similar scale or on similar lines.

Greywood was the vision and creation of one man, primarily for his own enjoyment. If others enjoyed working on the Railway or visiting it, that was simply a by-product of its existence and not the reason for it. Despite the hierarchy of officers to whom, to be sure, a degree of responsibility was delegated, Greywood's direction still smacked much more of an autocracy than a democracy, hardly surprising in view of the way operation of the line was funded by Sir John personally and quite independently of any 'fares revenue'. This attitude was exemplified by the timetable used in the latter years of Greywood's existence. If a train was booked to run at say, 4.32pm, it ran at 4.32 irrespective of whether there were passengers aboard or not.

The two Railways, not surprisingly, have many similarities, but it is in the role the public plays that there is an increasingly wide divergence of attitude. And it was probably the failure to appreciate this at the original planning stage that led to the difficulties under discussion.

While direct control of the Railway at Chertsey was vested in a Managing Committee of senior staff under Ian Allan's chairmanship, a company already existed within the Ian Allan Group for the purpose of operating miniature railways in a commercially-based environment. Though these lines were later disposed of, the GCR slotted neatly into this niche for it was decided that the eventual aim was to make the Railway self-funding, recovering its running costs and, perhaps, some capital expenditure out of accrued revenue. This immediately implied that the levels of passenger carryings needed to be very substantially higher than those ever contemplated at Greywood.

To meet these aims, so far as was possible without contravening

Above: The line's larger than scale 0-4-0 diesel mechanical locomotive *Thunderbolt* driven by Ian Allan heads through the country near Fork Junction with a mixed train of bogie and four-wheel stock

planning consent, the Railway had to be brought to the attention of the public. People had to be persuaded to visit in relatively large numbers and be encouraged to ride and pay for doing so. And, most importantly, the visit had to be made enjoyable and interesting enough to ensure those visitors not only came again but would publicise the Railway in conversation and correspondence. It would not be true to say that the Railway's survival depended solely on meeting commercial criteria but there was no doubt that funding on the lines of Greywood would not be continued indefinitely from Ian Allan Group resources.

One can question, with the undoubted benefit of hindsight, whether these goals and the steps required to achieve them were ever spelled out at the beginning or indeed whether they became formulated quite so categorically. One can also question whether the Committee members with these criteria before them would have designed the layout they did despite having little or no breadth of experience beyond Greywood to guide them. What they produced was, in effect, an enlarged and uncoiled version of Greywood quite unsuited to the close-headway, high-throughput service ultimately required. The Committee meeting that October evening in 1971 was faced with finding a way out of the dilemma that would not take too long to put into effect, nor would entail radical or wholesale changes in the existing layout. The major problem was posed, of course, by the still large proportion of single track. True double track only existed between Phillips Bridge and Fork Junction, at the immediate approach to Hardwick and in Everglades station. All single track was traversed in both directions. This limited headways and, thereby, track capacity with the result that much time was wasted by trains waiting at signals.

There was total agreement on what had to be done — doubling of as much single track as possible — but argument and counter-argument swayed over what form the changes should take and how they should be implemented. By the end of the evening the Committee had adopted a characteristically bold solution to the problem.

Priority was to be given to doubling the heavily-used Everglades Loop and making the Spur an entirely independent line between Everglades and Phillips Bridge. Doubling would, of course, render the crossovers at Fork Junction redundant so the points could be recovered for use elsewhere. At Hardwick provision of a new engine release line would allow the existing one to be used as a fourth platform road.

Much work had gone into the 'Phase 2' spiral, evidenced by the high embankment raised in 1967. But as it ran contrary to the aims now before the Committee, and the planned connections to it in Everglades station promised to make a difficult operating situation worse, it was decided to abandon this projected route.

The need for some longer-term planning was agreed upon too, a schedule of development to be tackled over the succeeding five years being worked out. This included the building of a new branch line as opportunity offered.

Inspection showed that the construction of a line exactly parallel to the southern half of the loop over Piggery Summit required major engineering work. One or both of two large oak trees near Fork Junction would have to be removed as there was insufficient loading-gauge clearance for two tracks to pass between them. But this problem was secondary to that presented by the infill needed to accommodate a second track on the embankment around and through the Pig Pond.

The Committee decided this part of the layout had to be operational by the time the 1972 season opened. But it was conceded the embankment would be impossible to build up and have settled, stabilised and ready for use within the limited time available. Instead, the line was routed alongside the opposite edge of the pond and then taken approximately parallel to, but at a little distance from, the existing track, joining up with the northern half of the loop through Pig Pond Cutting near Fork Junction and avoiding the problem of the Oak trees too. (In the event, one of the trees was felled during a violent thunderstorm in July 1982, struck by lightning that 'earthed' through the track, seriously damaging the Railway's power signalling equipment)

At this point the planners hit another snag. Nothing could disguise the fact that the connections to the new alignment at the Everglades end could only be made at the cost of some unacceptably sharp curvature if there was to be no conflict with the line into Pig Pond Cutting. The solution involved the abandonment of the cutting and the construction of another new route. This runs parallel to the outside of the spiral embankment before curving away to a junction with the southern section of the loop at Fork Junction. Earthworks for this line promised to be minimal.

It was estimated that all these changes would provide more than enough work for the coming winter but there remained the problem of the reversible line on the Polish Corridor to be dealt with before the full benefit of the changes could be seen. However not much could be done about this immediately for the construction and commissioning of a new embankment to carry the Spur directly from Everglades to Phillips Bridge was needed to eliminate it. And it was reckoned this would take a full year to accomplish.

Work on the additions at Hardwick began before the turn of the year and as soon as the plans for the new loco release arrangements had been finalised. The long siding cut into the bank behind the carriage shed formed the basis for these; the course for its extension involved removal of part of the raised banking approach and site of the small turntable from the original layout plan. Spoil from this was taken out to The Causeway where, in the new scheme for Everglades, the West end of the embankment required some widening and slight realignment. On 14 November the point recovered from the Down end at Phillips Bridge was set in place in the Up line at Hardwick to give a trailing connection from the new loco headshunt, while approaching the year's end the siding alongside the carriage shed was lifted prior to reballasting and relaying with dual-gauge Bassetts Manor track. The area for the headshunt itself had been cleared and levelled at the same time; the track, with the buffer-stops hard up against the Eastern boundary fence of the compound, was not laid in nor the connection to the point in the Up line made until the middle of February. The ultimate connection to the extended siding to complete the new runround had to wait another week.

The steadily growing number of people who had visited the Railway during the summer had shown up another shortcoming. Accommodation for those visitors who merely wished to watch the trains was very limited. To relieve some of the overcrowding in the circulating area which resulted from this situation the triangular piece of land alongside the Hardwick Lane fence, bounded by the turntable and the containers, was cleared of undergrowth at the beginning of the year and fenced as a viewing area.

This was seen as a short-term solution but plans for other viewing areas within the main field have always foundered on safety of access. Nevertheless, another, temporary, site at the top of Hardwick Bank, between the Main and Spur lines and reached by a policed foot crossing, was opened in 1984.

Out in the main field meanwhile, work on the new line to supersede the route through Pig Pond Cutting got under way in February. As anticipated, construction of the alignment, named 'Meadowside', was straightforward and required only two afternoon's work to see the trackbed complete and ready to accept track recovered from the cutting. This was put in on 2 April, ballasting being completed two weeks later.

The new Up route — the 'Jungle' line — proved rather more difficult, needing widening of part of The Causeway and the excavation of a shallow cutting through the same ridge on which Piggery Summit stands. It also cut off a small part of the pond which meant that another drainage pipe had to be provided under the track at the Up end of Everglades station.

As noted spoil for The Causeway widening mainly came from the works in Hardwick yard but it was supplemented by some of the material dug out of the shallow Jungle line cutting. Progress during January and February was steady rather than spectacular but by the end of that period, and despite heavy rain which had caused severe flooding of the ditches alongside it once more, only turfing was required to finish off the widened embankment. This was done in April. Track was laid in the new formation from Fork Junction through the Jungle to the site of the new culvert at Everglades following completion of the cutting at the beginning of that same month, and it had been ballasted by 23 April. Work on the culvert itself was carried out a week later, the cutting having provided spoil for packing up and over the pipes to form the roadbed. That same day the track was put in place across it and connection made to the point in the Down Main where the line diverged at the Down end of Everglades station. Some realignment of track at the entrance end of the ballast siding became necessary as a result of the layout alterations and this work was done on 7 May, which permitted a consignment of ballast filling the concourse at Hardwick to be worked into the storage area before the scheduled opening of the season.

The Fork Junction crossovers were lifted on 5 March. One point was used for the convergence of the Jungle and Meadowside lines while another temporarily formed a part of the Spur. This allowed a short siding to be taken off it at what was to become the head of the new alignment to Phillips Bridge so that trains of spoil to raise the embankment for that line could be berthed and unloaded without interfering with main line services. After 11 June, when this siding was installed, spoil workings featured strongly on operating days as well as on alternate Sundays when the Railway was closed to the public.

As on other works of this kind, however, the bank grew very slowly despite this concerted effort, until a visit from a JCB on 16 July finished off the job in a single afternoon. It took spoil mainly from the area South of the new alignment, causing a considerable enlargement of the pond that had formed after excavations for material to build the shallow embankment at Phillips Bridge. As is typical of the gravel subsoil, the new excavations soon filled with water. Due to motorway construction in the vicinity since then the water level has fallen dramatically.

The opening of the 1972 season saw yet another serious derailment of one of the articulated units on points. It finished up on its side having turned over, it was established, mainly as a result of passengers leaning out through the curve. Injuries were minor and the stock returned to service following a cursory examination which found nothing was broken or too badly bent. But there is evidence in retrospect that these sets were responsible for a rising trend of derailments over the following seasons. Questions began to be asked about the suitability of the cast-frame bogies for the heavy demands made on them, most coming from drivers whose engines were finding it increasingly difficult to haul stock equipped with them. Various remedies to ease matters were tried but the problem was only resolved when 'standard' bogies were fitted.

No other work was attempted on the Spur during the rest of the season, the embankment being left to settle and consolidate. In the autumn things got under way again: indeed, October 1972 might well have been christened 'Concrete Month.' The engineers laid the platforms in the 'V' of the Down Main and Up Jungle lines at Everglades as well as casting the signalbox steps, and putting in the new platform 4 at Hardwick.

The loop at Everglades was lengthened at its Up end in November, a new, larger-radius dural point being cut into the Down Main in rear of the steel one, which was removed. As experience showed that the extra distance from the box would make the 'pull' too long to be accomplished successfully off the short-throw levers in the main frame, a redundant two-lever fog-frame was purchased from BR. To take advantage of the pull this generated the Mechanical Engineer devised a new type of point machine that had a locking mechanism contained within it. This was set in place beside the point on Christmas Eve 1972; by the end of January the fog-frame had been installed in the box and the wire connection run from it.

As part of the arrangements for the new Spur the three roads at Phillips Bridge were reduced to two, with a trailing crossover between them to carry trains off the Spur to the Down Main. Lifting track and removal of the paved platforms and ballast took most of February 1973. The new alignments were pegged out and the track laid roughly in position early in March though ballasting did not commence until a substantial number of sleepers had been replaced. The track was ballasted and fettled by the end of April though edging up along the trackbed sides to retain the ballast in place and concreting in the posts for the new signals to control the layout went on into May, by which time attention had turned to the Spur.

A survey at the end of April finally determined the gradients on the new embankment; as usual, pegs fixed track height and line. The bank had been built up well above the projected level of the trackbed to save time and labour in raising the edges to retain the ballast when the track was in place. This paid dividends now despite the slight lessening of the overall height through settlement and compaction of the material. Cutting a ballast channel along the crown of the bank was initiated on 29 April and continued on into June, though after the season opened only as and when staff could be spared on days when the Railway operated. The first lengths of track were positioned at the foot of the bank on 1 July and connected to the point that had been removed from the original Spur Junction and relaid during the Spring as part of the new Phillips Bridge layout. By the middle of July the track extended right through to Everglades due to some intensive work by a small but experienced team. Operation during the 1973 season while all this was going on had reverted to a simple 'out-and-back' run via Piggery summit and Meadowside. But the Spur was reopened for Down trains on 29 July as soon as ballasting had been finished. The 'R1', under extreme caution, headed the first train through in mid-afternoon. Commissioning two weeks later of the point motor and five new colour-light signals covering the Phillips Bridge area, but controlled from a 'panel' in Everglades Junction box, permitted initiation of a full service in both directions to bring all the redesigned layout into use. From that time too the operating schedule was stepped up from fortnightly to weekly.

The new arrangements together, which saw the main line section of the Railway as it is today complete, were all that had been hoped of them, providing much increased track capacity over that of the original layout and a far greater degree of operational flexibility.

EXTENSION: Branch to Cockcrow Hill

Above: Looking East across the railway from near Everglades Junction in 1976 . The three lines in view are (from left to right) the Spur, the branch with a 'contractors' track in place from the new point in the foreground, and Meadowside, curving sharply away to the right. This view is now completely obscured by the subsequent growth of trees and other vegetation.

The next phase of development, decided upon at the previous year's committee meeting, dominated discussion at the one in November 1972. It centred on the proposal to construct a branch line as a long-term project. But since necessary main line maintenance could not be neglected, this would be worked on only as and when the opportunity arose.

The Committee also decided that, although mapping out the route itself formed a necessary preliminary to construction, the detailed planning of each phase would not be attempted until the previous one had been completed or was nearly so. This turned out to be a wise move.

A narrow tongue of land forming a continuation of The Copse had been acquired along the east side of the stream as part of the Title to the main field. The original proposal envisaged making use of this land for a route out to a small terminus at the foot of the western slope of Cockcrow Hill.

The line would have diverged from the Down Main just before Bishops Culvert and followed the stream closely thence. But the terminus site proved to be not nearly as remote from the main line as the Committee had hoped or would have liked. Clearance of the trees and undergrowth from it only promised to emphasise this. And because the branch would have been relatively short it was concluded that the journey would probably be unattractive to passengers. So other possibilities were explored.

The most promising route diverged at the Down end of Everglades on a curving embankment leading to a viaduct crossing the main line and the stream just East of the culvert and then following the originally proposed route. Though this would not solve the remoteness issue, it would give a longer run and bring the junction directly under the eye of the Everglades signalman.

It was also suggested that the original proposal for a divergence from the Down Main should be put in for Down direction services, leaving the route over the viaduct for Up trains only.

But this whole proposition foundered when a preliminary survey showed that the gradient between ground level at the terminus and the viaduct would need to be unacceptably steep to achieve the required clearances. So interest switched instead to the eastern side of Cockcrow Hill where another small triangle of land was available.

The collective imagination of the staff produced numerous schemes for this area, in the main variations on two basic themes. The more modest postulated a Down Main junction at Phillips Bridge and a separate crossing of the stream below the existing bridge to a terminus at the extreme East end of the triangle.

Return routes varied. The most basic simply used the same single track with trains passing through the crossover at the foot of the Spur to gain the Up line. Another envisaged a line skirting the northern slope of the hill to rejoin the Down Main by Bishops Culvert. The most ambitious made use of the 'embankment/viaduct' technique to bridge the main line and stream and bring the track across the field to a junction at Everglades.

The second basic theme made use of a circular route. This line diverged from the Down Main at the culvert and passed through the wooded area beside the stream to circumnavigate the hill. It then crossed the stream and the main line near Phillips Bridge before proceeding on embankment to a junction at Everglades.

Variations included a clockwise circuit — from the Down Main at Phillips Bridge and round the hill to rejoin the line at Fork Junction — and from the same starting point and over the same route but then crossing the stream and main line by the culvert and continuing on embankment to Everglades. Any decision to pursue a line on this theme had to be conditional upon land being made available on the hill.

In view of this last point an arrangement on the lines of the first theme found more general favour. Nobody would have readily passed up the idea of a long run around the hill but the less ambitious scheme was clearly the most practical.

After long consideration the plan that finally emerged was the last-mentioned of the three variations. By taking advantage of the slope of the hill, which is more pronounced along the eastern side, it was found that a gradient of 1 in 70 from existing ground level at the terminus would provide adequate headroom beneath a viaduct over the Main lines.

The idea of separate Down and Up lines began to lose favour, for this reinstatement of 'token working' over a single track, which had ended with the closure of Phillips bridge box, promised to add another degree of interest to the Railway. It also reflected the general belief that traffic would be light. Moreover, the suggested Down Branch divergence further lost popularity because it entailed another crossing downstream of Phillips Bridge.

Construction of the embankment East of Everglades Junction had already been started when two more small pieces of land were acquired in exchange for the ground alongside the stream. These brought the area available for branch development up to some ⅓ of a hectare or ⅘ acre.

One of these pieces allowed a widening of the original triangle while the other permitted extension of the branch further out into the country. This promised to make the terminus really remote from the main line, a feeling heightened by the level crossing that would be necessary at its immediate approaches to give farm vehicles and animals access to the fields on the other side of the line. But at the same time the extended and enlarged area now available caused the idea of a second line from the terminus to the Down Main at Bishops Culvert to come back into prominence. Arguments for and against it were resolved by agreement on a compromise. In this, the Branch would be completed as a single track only and the construction of a return line was then to be pursued only if traffic levels warranted it. But the cutting for it would be excavated anyway to provide material for the embankment leading down to the terminus.

The building of the branch as first conceived fell naturally into three phases. But the change of circumstances caused by the extra land provided two more. Chronologically, the five were:-

i. Raising and grading the embankment between Everglades and the stream and laying a 'contractors' railway for carrying materials and equipment for phase ii.

ii. Bridging the stream and the main line, a span of 15m.

iii. Raising and grading the embankment between the viaduct and site of the level crossing.

iv. Construction of the level crossing and provision of the associated fencing.

v. Laying out of the branch terminus.

A time scale of five years had originally been projected to see construction finished; optimistic hopes were expressed that this completion period could be maintained even with the additional work provided by the extension of the site. At the same time nobody was under any illusions about priorities. Building the branch did not often figure at the top of the list and this is reflected in the overrun of the constructional period by a full year. It is agreed without demur though that the result of the project made the time taken to complete it wholly worthwhile.

A start was made before the end of 1973 on building up the Phase i embankment, initially by barrowing spoil from 'The Quarry', an aptly-named part of the high, obsolete 'spiral' bank alongside the Jungle line. By the beginning of the 1974 season the engineers had all of five metres of new embankment to show for their winter-long efforts! With something in the order of 90m required in all, exceeding three metres above existing ground level in places, building the lot by this method was clearly out of the question. But a hand-worked point, properly clipped to prevent accidental or unauthorised movement of the blades, was installed in the Meadowside line where the new alignment diverged from it and a track laid along this stub of embankment. Thereafter, several wagon-loads of spoil were hauled from the Quarry on summer Sundays as time permitted, though not while the Railway was open to the public. In fact, it was not until November that the final line of the embankment was settled and a full survey fixing heights had to wait until June. The following month a JCB came in to raise the new bank.

The survey had provided for a minimum 1.5m clearance above railhead where the branch crossed the main line near Phillips Bridge. This required the embankment to be built on a rising gradient over ground that steadily falls away beneath it. As a result the JCB could only just reach the highest point, on the approach to the viaduct, where the bank stands over 3m high.

Most of the spoil was skimmed off the surrounding ground to a depth of about 30cm. As in earlier works of this kind the bank was left to settle through the winter though, as it turned out, little work was attempted on it until the spring of 1976, after the viaduct itself had been constructed.

The final method to be used for bridging the stream and the main line had not been decided upon until the summer of 1975. One idea pursued quite seriously was to use two large-diameter concrete pipes, to run the main lines through, as well as a smaller one for culverting the stream. But this foundered upon the basic problems of transporting and handling such unwieldy objects.

It was finally agreed to build a girder bridge which, by its nature, can be prefabricated and moved easily for erection on site.

Digging out the foundations for the piers and the two intermediate supports began before the end of the 1975 season. Because of the alluvial nature of the subsoil and the proximity of the stream these foundations were designed to spread their load over as wide an area as possible. The one beside the Down road was poured first, at the end of November, and by the beginning of December the pier on it was almost up to height.

A week later, the foundation for the intermediate support by the Up road had been poured and, despite heavy rain at the turn of the year, the other two foundations were complete by 11 January 1976. By the end of the month the stream-side pier was up to height.

These piers consist of hollow concrete blocks that, for the first three courses, are set over reinforcing rods embedded in the foundations. After more rods had been inserted from above to full height, the cores of the blocks were filled with concrete.

Meanwhile, work had been going ahead on the platforms at Hardwick on prefabricating the steelwork, welding being used very extensively in the construction. Materials consisted of six 12.5cm RSJ girders for the main spans with channel, angle and square tubing for the intermediate supports and piping for handrails. Much of it had been obtained as scrap and required rust removal and subsequent painting with an inhibitor before any assembly work could be done.

Below: Steelwork for the branch line viaduct takes shape at Hardwick prior to being shifted into position - a mammoth undertaking.

To join the girders together in such a way as to make assembly on site a straightforward task, steel plates were welded each side of the web at the end of an RSJ and bolted to the web of the adjoining one; there were four such sets of couplings. In addition, lugs for the handrail stanchions were welded on both top and bottom flanges and holes drilled through the web to accept the reinforcing rods for the concrete floor. The intermediate supports, usually termed 'A frames' because the legs splay outwards, were fabricated entirely by welding using channel section and angle girders cross-braced by tubing.

Handrails were made out of piping of two diameters, the larger one being used as stanchions, the smaller for the rails themselves. Steel discs on the lugs on the lower flanges of the main girders fit snugly into the stanchions, which are held in place by bolts through the lugs on the upper flanges. The spans, when complete and in primer paint, were broken down again into six sections on 1 February, and moved out to the site itself by rail the following weekend. With an experienced team on the job the girders were erected in a single afternoon though the handrails were not run through the stanchions until the end of the month.

With the main steelwork in position it only remained to level it up with jacks and packing so that the concrete plinths on which the A frames rest could be shuttered and poured, a job completed on 15 February. That weekend also saw track being put into place on the new embankment.

Much of this track consisted of rail recovered from the commercial company, turned because of flange wear and laid on new sleepers. The line was finished early in March. The primary object of laying it was to transport the material for the reinforced concrete deck of the viaduct.

Erecting the scaffolding and shuttering, putting the reinforcing rods and netting in place and 'floating' the floor over the usual polythene membrane occupied the bridge team over five weeks from the end of March. On production line principles, the concrete was dry-mixed at Hardwick and railed out to the site where water was added.

The scaffolding over the main line was still in place when the 1976 season opened at the beginning of May but proper 'hazard warning' boards ensured there were no cracked heads. In fact, even though there is more than enough clearance passengers still tend to duck instinctively as they pass beneath the viaduct. Digging out and laying the foundations for the wing walls and the latter's construction using cored concrete blocks had begun at the end of February and continued throughout March though, with little urgency attached to the job because of other work, the walls and the capping to their piered ends were not finally completed until a year later, in April 1977.

As usual, little was done during summer but throughout the following 1976 winter the 'Quarry' on the Jungle line again became the source of innumerable wagon-loads of spoil. These were tipped to raise the sides of the embankment, which had sunk appreciably since its construction, to form the ballast trough and to widen the top of the bank near the viaduct where the difficulty experienced by the JCB in reaching this high point had left it rather narrow. The bank was surveyed again in mid-February 1977. By the beginning of March ballasting the track had begun from the Everglades and, despite some very wet weather and time spent completing the wing walls of the viaduct, the whole length had been coarse-ballasted by the time the season opened at the beginning of May.

With the additional pieces of land now available to extend the branch beyond its original limits the third phase of construction work was initiated in July when the section to the level crossing was surveyed and pegged out for line and height. At the same time a rough survey fixed the line of the cutting to supply spoil for the embankment. The JCB came in on 6 August and the bank was roughly graded the following day. But, as before, no other work on it was attempted until settlement had taken place.

Towards the end of September preliminary work began on clearing and marking out the site of the level crossing and erecting the gate posts at its four corners. Building the crossing itself began after the 1977 season had come to an end, when work started on digging out its 4.25m square area to depths ranging from 20cm to 40cm. Spoil was distributed along the embankment towards the viaduct.

The deepest sections are around the sides of the square and beneath the track; these 'beams' were poured first, during three weekends in December. Filling in the shallower sections and bedding-in the steel track lengths over the crossing had been completed by the middle of January. A week later, after the fencing had been rearranged, the crossing was made available for farm traffic.

A little over 12 tonnes of concrete, all mixed by hand, had been required. And because a gap was needed in the embankment to allow animals and farm vehicles free movement until the crossing was ready, all the materials had to be barrowed 80m to the site from a dump by the viaduct. The gap in the embankment was closed at the beginning of February from a spoil heap left handily for the purpose and during the course of the next month the track was installed over the length between the viaduct and the crossing. In the middle of March the JCB paid a further visit to level off the site of Cockcrow Hill station, which had a very pronounced slope from one side to the other. As in previous years, however, the necessity of handling the ever-increasing traffic on summer Sundays during 1978 caused suspension of any constructional work there until the autumn, though the track was extended into the station area in April. A series of ballast trains worked down on to this section of the branch on the night of 4 November after the Bonfire Night traffic had ceased. Excavations for Cockcrow Hill signalbox commenced two weeks after that.

The box is dug into the hillside so that its southern wall is sunk over 1.5m below track level. Spoil from the site was taken away by rail and tipped along the embankment beyond the crossing and The Causeway to repair some slippage. Pouring the concrete floor began in mid-December but ragbolting down the new lever frame, laying in a waterproof membrane and screeding up to the requisite level occupied the rest of the month and the whole of January.

Attention then turned to construction of the turntable pit. This one is much shallower than that at Hardwick but a considerable amount of spoil had to be dug out from the uphill side of the circle. Concreting the floor and accurately setting in the post for the central bearing had been completed by 1 April though the circular brick retaining wall was not put in for another month. By the beginning of May too the walls of the signalbox had been completed and the roof was in place a week later. As usual, concrete blocks were used for this building with a flat timber and felt-covered roof. The short flight of steps down to the door of the box had been fashioned early in February together with the digging of a soakaway at their foot, but cementing and bricking the treads did not take place until June.

In June too a runround loop was installed at the branch terminus so that a limited passenger service could be started. The ex-Greywood North turntable, suitably refurbished, went in on 15 July and by the end of the month the three tracks in the layout had been connected up to it: a full service was initiated on 5 August 1979.

Continued on page 27

Below: The completed girders of the viaduct newly in position, spanning the stream and the main line. Cockcrow Hill rises behind them.

THE LOCOMOTIVE STUD

1 North Eastern Railway Class 'R1' 4-4-0 No.1239, built in 1913 by F W Baldwin Brothers and painted in NER 'pea-green' lined livery.

2 London & North Eastern Railway Class 'K5' 2-6-0 No.206, built in 1956 by Phillip Simpson, Dick Simmonds and Fred Stone. is seen in LNER war-time lined black livery.

3 A freelance GCR-type 4-6-2 No.1947 *'Eureka'*, built in 1927 by Louis Shaw, in unlined Brunswick green livery.

4 LNER Class 'K3' 2-6-0 No.1935, built 1974 by Hugh Saunders. is seen in LNER lined 'apple-green' livery.

5 This Southern Railway Class 'S15' 4-6-0 No.837, was built in 1947 by David Curwen and painted in SR lined olive-green livery.

6 A War Department Class 'WD' 2-10-0 No.73755, built in 1951 by J N Liversage is pictured in 'desert sand' livery but can now be seen finished in typical WD khaki-grey.

7 BR. Class '7MT' 4-6-2 No.70020, *'Mercury'*, built 1985 by Norman Sleet. pictured in BR. lined Brunswick green livery. A further three BR '7MT' Class engines are currently under construction, Nos. 70047 (to be named *Lady of the Lake*) and 70054, *Dornoch Firth*, by John Butt and Kim Richardson respectively, and one to be named, by Norman Sleet.

8 There are two LMS Class '8F' 2-8-0's, No. 8374, built in 1993 by Hancock & York, and No. 8200, built by Pownall of Kingsbridge in 1984. Both are in LMS goods unlined black livery.

9 Two LMS Class '5MT' 4-6-0's run on the line, No. 5145, built in 1988 by Norman Sleet, and No. 5000 *'Sister Dora'*, built by Arthur Glaze in 1981, Both appear in LMS lined black livery. No .45440 is currently under construction by Jeremy Clarke and will be turned out in BR mixed traffic black livery.

10 There are three examples of the London Midland & Scottish Railway Class '6P' (*'Royal Scot'*) 4-6-0. No.6100 *'Royal Scot'* was built by John Butt in 1981 and is seen in LMS 1927 lined red livery. An earlier example of this same loco was built in 1947 by Cecil Barnett and Len Willoughby, and No. 6115 *'Scots Guardsman'* was completed in 1989 by Peter Almond. These two engines are in LMS maroon livery.

11 NER Class 'T2' 0-8-0 No.1249, *'Hecate'*, built in 1986 by Roger Sills is pictured in NER lined black goods livery.

12 A Great Western Railway Class 6959 (Modified Hall) 4-6-0 No.7915, *'Mere Hall'*, built in 1952 by Rowe of Welwyn and painted in British Railways lined Brunswick green livery.

13 GWR '1400' Class 0-4-2T No.1401, built in 1980 by Roger Sills and sporting BR unlined black livery.

14 This SR (ex-LBSCR) Class 'H2' 4-4-2 No.2422, *'North Foreland'* was built by Jamie Lester in 1981 and painted in SR lined olive-green livery.

15 Southern Railway Merchant Navy Class 4-6-2 No.21C11, *'General Steam Navigation'* is seen in SR lined malachite green livery and was built in 1993 by Norman Sleet and Michael Lester. A similar SR Battle of Britain Class 4-6-2, No. 34051, *'Winston Churchill'*, was completed by Norman Sleet in 1995. It appears in BR Brunswick Green livery.

16 'Hymek' Bo-Bo battery-powered electric, *'A B MacLeod'*, was built in 1982 by Arthur Glaze in lined brown livery.

17 This BR Class '40' 1Co-Co1 diesel electric No.40 106 was built 1993 by Norman Sleet. It has a lawn mower engine with hydraulic drive, and is painted in BR unlined Brunswick green livery.

18 An LMS 0-6-0 diesel-shunter No.11, *'Faraday'*, (ex-*Winifred*), built in 1958 by Jennings and Marsden for A B MacLeod. It is powered by a 50cc Honda petrol engine with 4-speed gearbox and mechanical drive via a jackshaft, and is seen in unlined BR Brunswick green livery.

Rolling Stock

Above: The level crossing at Cockcrow Hill sees a train from Hardwick Central, headed by the GWR 'Hall' Class 4-6-0 No.7915, *Mere Hall*, coasting downgrade from the viaduct in 1984.

Right: The first course of blocks to form the walls of the Up Branch line tunnel is in place and being pointed in 1985. The construction train is headed by electric locomotive *A B MacLeod*. The M25 can be seen in the background.

Paved platforms were in place at Cockcrow Hill for the start of the 1980 season but the exposed nature of the site highlighted the need for a shelter for passengers in inclement weather. The signalbox was used in such emergencies for two seasons but this obviously was not a long-term solution. In December 1981 therefore the prefabricated concrete shed that had served as the signalbox at Phillips Bridge Junction was transported out to the branch terminus in sections and re-erected with a new, canopied roofline on the Down side platform over two weekends in April.

Lingering doubts that the branch might attract only light traffic were dispelled as soon as it opened. The fact that the turntable and full station layout were not completed until the middle of the season and engines made the return trip tender first as a result — indeed, for the first month or so of operation only one train at a time could be accommodated beyond Everglades — did not deter passengers at all. Before the 1980 season was out traffic on the branch exceeded that on the circuit, a situation that continued for several years. Capacity on the long single line became seriously stretched and it was not unusual for a harassed Everglades

signalman to put a Down branch train 'into orbit' while a laggard Up service cleared the section. In these circumstances it was decided at the 1982 Committee meeting to proceed with the construction of an Up branch line. It was also decided to attempt to work a tunnel into its length somewhere, a feature at Greywood that had not yet appeared at Chertsey.

Some misgivings were expressed over pressing ahead with the original scheme, for under it Up direction branch trains would be fed into the Down line at Bishops Culvert to pass over the steeply graded and already heavily-used section thence to Everglades. A number of other options aimed at avoiding this situation came under consideration at the same meeting. In one of these there arose, Phoenix-like, the idea of a new Down line diverging at Phillips Bridge to a separate downstream crossing and then running roughly parallel to the embankment. This would have required the existing branch line to be severed and slewed over to join the unused track on the level crossing to take Up services, releasing the other for use by the new line. The disadvantage of this scheme was that a tunnel would not be possible given the lie of the land in that area and so a second scheme was worked out. In this the divergence left the Down line immediately at the Down end of Phillips Bridge to curve sharply under the existing branch and through the higher ground beyond it before emerging to join the incipient cutting at the approach to the level crossing. The short piece of 'Right-hand running' which would result was considered acceptable in these circumstances.

The proposed line was pegged out early in 1983 and a rough survey made of the necessary levels before circumstances conspired to change the decision. Once more the question of time available to complete a project came to the fore. The tunnel was to be built on the 'cut and cover' principle, that is, a deep trench would be dug out along the line and to the required depth of the tunnel. After the walls and roof had been constructed the original land contours would be built up using spoil recovered from the excavations. In this '1982 scheme' the tunnel would, of course, cut through the existing branch line embankment and there was some doubt as to whether it would be possible to complete this part of the work satisfactorily before the start of the 1983 season given other maintenance commitments. There was also the problem of having to fell a large tree which stood four-square across the line just beyond the divergence from the Down Main at Phillips Bridge and grub out its massive roots. Taking these things into consideration it was reluctantly decided to revert to the originally planned route via the Culvert, and if traffic over the Down Main became too congested as a result to reinstate single-line working while other possibilities were explored.

This new route was pegged out in September 1983, with one slight deviation from the line of the rough cutting, so that a survey fixing

1 NER Class 'T2' 0-8-0 *'Hecate'* stands at Cockcrow Hill at the head of a freight train from Hardwick Central. The vehicles (from the engine) are: GCR brake van No.9, tank wagon No.1, bogie bolster No. 43, 'Loco coal' wagon No.53, a 'riding' wagon, sand wagon No.7, bogie Engineers Hopper No.41, the second 'riding' wagon, and LMS brake van No.8 at the rear.

2 With steam to spare after the climb to Piggery Summit, '8F' No.8200 runs briskly along the Down Loop with a freight train at Everglades Junction. The vehicles are: G C brake No.9, 'crocodile' No.48, 'open' No.35, 'riding' No.52, 'sand' No.7, then three tanker wagons Nos.1, 46, and 45, followed by 'open' No.73, 'bolster' No.43 (with a load of rails), 'riding' No.51 and lastly an LMS brake No.8 bringing up the rear.

3 Ex-Greywood carriage no. 122 equipped with standard bogies. Note shallower body and angled ends of the foot well compared to the standard stock.

4 Ex-Greywood articulated unit, carriages 101 and 102, equipped with standard roller-bearing bogies.

5 Standard carriage No. 136 finished in Pullman livery and named *'Annette'*.

6 Standard prototype carriage no. 124, built in 1976.

heights could be made and presented to the committee for consideration at the annual meeting early in November. The proposals were agreed and, aided by a mild winter, work proceeded apace. Despite having to deepen the existing cutting by up to 30cm in places, the section between the level crossing and the convergence at Bishops Culvert had been completed with partly turfed and uniformly 'battered' sides, which enhanced its appearance quite considerably, by the beginning of January 1984. The soil dug out during this exercise was piled up alongside the deepest part of the cutting to await construction of the tunnel during the 1984/5 winter. Work of a more urgent nature precluded this however, though the footings were dug out and filled with brick rubble at the end of March 1985 and the concrete foundations for the 20m-long walls were poured during the last two weekends in April. The first two courses of concrete blocks were laid in over several Sundays during the 1985 season and the remainder in November that year to provide the standard 1.5m clearance above track level. Most of the roof is made of ex-BR sleepers laid transversely and these were in place by the year end. The tunnel mouths are of 'Egyptian Arch' profile which extends one and a half metres in from each end. A former for these sections was set on the block walls and the profiles turned over it in brick. The Cockcrow Hill end was completed first and when the brick work had set the former was removed and reset at the western end. The brick portals and wing walls were not completed until the 1986 season opened in May. But in March the earth covering was built up and landscaped, some 200 tons of soil being required to provide a 'natural' land profile. Since then the growth of trees and vegetation disguises the artificiality of this feature completely. The 100m of new track in the line, including the point in the Down Main by the culvert, had been laid in and ballasted by the end of February 1984. Nearly 70m of this track was brand new 'Fenlow', the remainder coming from a small stock of lightly-used 'Bassets Manor' track acquired in 1981.

Signalling changes in connection with the new line had been started during the 1983 summer with the installation of a new Down Main signal to protect the convergence. It came into operation in June. Major alterations to the arrangements at Cockcrow Hill and on the single line itself were clearly out of the question until the close of the season but the bases for the Up Advanced Starter — an electrically worked semaphore controlled by Cockcrow Hill box — and the Up direction colour-light Distant and Stop signal posts on the approach to the convergence at the culvert were in place by November together with the associated cabling from a new relay cabinet located at the junction. By the end of January the post for the 'Everglades Up Home' colour-light on the existing single line had been relocated on the Down side to support a new automatic Advanced Starter signal.

As an additional attraction both for passengers and staff, it was also agreed at the 1983 Committee Meeting to make further attempts to run a freight train regularly during the summer when conditions permitted. Basing freight operation at Hardwick had already proved impractical. But with the doubling of the branch it seemed most of the problems could be resolved by running the train around the circuit to and from Cockcrow Hill instead. Partly for this purpose a new upside loop in the terminus layout was surveyed, pegged and troughed out at the end of January, though it was another month before the track and points at each end of it had been laid and ballasted.

The signalling and point lever connections in the area were altered to give access to the loop directly off the existing loco release road, which would also serve as an arrival line for the freight train. The Branch rises on a gradient of 1 in 200 between the level crossing and the station throat, but as the loop would hold unbraked freight stock the resultant height difference of 12cm had to be absorbed entirely within a short distance at the Up end to permit the rest of the loop to be built on the level. A siding off the loop, with a slight gradient towards the buffer stops to prevent runaways, was laid in during April 1984.

Operation of the terminus proved a little restricted by the portion of bi-directional single track between the platforms and the divergence of the Up line near the level crossing. This became more pronounced as traffic built up but the layout, which clearly reflected the planning stage view that traffic would be light, survived for several seasons. Its redevelopment is discussed in a later chapter.

Left: In 1978 a short freight train ambles through The Copse toward Fork Junction headed by No.7915, *Mere Hall* driven by Richard Stokes.

Below: Pictured in 1979 during the short period before the Cockcrow Hill turntable was brought into commission 'S15' No.837 climbs away from the branch terminus tender-first bound for Hardwick Central.

Above right: The 'Gladesman', double-headed by class 'K5' No.206 and *'Eureka'* awaits departure time at Hardwick Central.

Above far right: On the occasion of its 80th birthday celebrations in 1993, the 'R1' 4-4-0 drifts through Everglades Junction hauling period 4-wheel stock. The artist Terence Cuneo sits immediately behind driver Eleanor Sills.

Below right: 'Royal Scot' arrives at Cockcrow Hill on a Down train. The driver is Alan Williams.

Above: The single-line is cleared by the 'diesel'-shunter *Winifred* (now named *Faraday*) as her driver, A B '*Mac*' MacLeod, hands the token from Cockcrow Hill to the Everglades Junction signalman in 1980. Mac's association with the GCR covered more than forty years. His influence was profound and still continues to the present.

Right: LMS '8F' 2-8-0 No.8200 tops the Spur on a circuit working in 1991. The electrically-worked semaphores were superseded by a 4-aspect colour-light signal in 1993.

Below: Quiet before the storm: Staff snatch a few minutes relaxation at Hardwick Central before a Sunday afternoon's operation begins in 1992, Locomotives on view are (left to right) an 8F, two Black Fives and the K5.

CONSOLIDATION: (i): To 1986

With the completion of the redesigned main line layout subsequent work, except that connected with construction of the branch, was almost all by way of providing new ancillary facilities or improving existing ones.

The first of these was undertaken concurrently with the latter stages of the layout alteration in anticipation of the provision of mains electricity on site. It involved laying an underground, multi-core ring main, carrying several voltages, right round the Railway with outlets at strategic points.

Concrete bases for junction boxes to accommodate the outlets were cast *in situ* in January 1973 and the first box was in place at Fork Junction that same month. The outlet at Phillips Bridge was housed in the erstwhile signalbox building.

As extension of power signalling progressed junction boxes appeared at Hardwick Central, Everglades Junction, Culvert Junction, Fork Junction and Phillips Bridge Junction.

The mains power supply was linked up by the Electricity Board at the end of 1973 and the faithful 'genny' returned to its owner shortly afterwards. The electricians on the staff have since installed numerous power points and enhanced lighting in the locomotive and carriage sheds at Hardwick as well as in the booking office, on the station platforms and at other strategic locations around the yard there. All three signalboxes have also been equipped with lights and mains outlets.

Mains power provided two other improvements. The first benefitted the staff directly, taking the form of an electric water storage heater, giving hot water on tap at a basin installed in the engine shed. This allowed a much more comfortable and dignified end to a day's work that the 'cat's lick and promise' under a water crane that had been the usual practice before.

The second improvement concerned water too. Unless the water tank was more than half full delivery at the cranes in the station and yard was very slow due to the lack of pressure. To counteract this, the outlet pipe was severed so that two 'T' pieces could be let into it. A branch pipe taken off one of these fed a header tank, the outlet from that feeding back into the other 'T' piece. A stop-cock on a short connection between the two permitted water to by-pass the header if required. An additional outlet with a handle-operated butterfly valve was provided on the header tank, for fast filling of watering cans, weedkilling tanks and so on.

The header, of 25l capacity, stood some 3.5m above the ground on a 15cm diameter cast iron pipe whose bottom end was set into a concrete-filled brick plinth. Water was raised by an electric pump operated on a contact system worked by the usual domestic ball-valve arrangement, the water line being enclosed within the supporting pipe. The tank was removed in 1995.

The header tank system allowed two water cranes to be installed beside the Down roads at Everglades Junction. This job required such extensive trenching that it took a three-month period to mid-February 1974 to complete. At the same time a branch was taken off this water line to another crane alongside the headshunt at Hardwick. This proved something of a mixed blessing as some drivers refused to move out of the headshunt until the tender was filled completely, despite the operational difficulties caused. The problem was not finally eradicated until the crane was removed in 1981 and a pair provided by the new ashpits.

Below: A B MacLeod, in its original green livery, at Cockcrow Hill level crossing with an arrival from Hardwick Central in 1993.

Construction of these pits reflected a change of emphasis on loco servicing. Much of it used to be done in the station area after engines had backed on to their trains. This resulted in a hotch-potch of coal hods and oilcans littering the platform ends, which detracted from the general appearance of the station. Track damage ensued where fires were cleaned and ashes dropped regularly.

The first ashpit was built in the 1980/1 close season, the second the following winter. Each is a concrete-floored depression some 25cm deep with a deeper, brick-lined trench beneath the track. This is made just wide enough to permit clearance of ashes from it with an ordinary domestic fire shovel. So that intermediate supports do not get in the way the track spans the pit on steel angle girders embedded in the top of the pit's concrete end walls; as the runround is curved at this point these girders had to be bent very accurately before positioning so as to follow properly the line of the curve. Grids beside the water cranes and the trenches themselves, in which the bricks forming the floor are laid loose on a ballast base without mortar, permit the drainage of water into a soakaway. The pits are open on the South side: this permitted the coal bins to be moved there during March 1982 from their somewhat inconvenient location against the end wall of the carriage shed.

Track changes out on the main line were few following the completion of the new layout. With the general build up of traffic during the 70s, the layout at Everglades proved rather restrictive. True, trains in the Down Main platform could be signalled across on to the Spur but this was a hangover from the days of the single line and passing loop layout there. So the opportunity was taken during the final phase of resignalling within the station area to put in a Down Loop to Down Main crossover, giving a much greater degree of operational flexibility. Installation work was carried out during February and March 1976, concurrently with the erection of a cantilever gantry to support the new colour-light starting signals.

The first subsequent change to track alignment took place within a year of the layout revision though it had been planned earlier. The curves at each end of The Copse were found to be rather severe, not so much as to warrant a very cautious approach but making no allowance for the unexpected. As a result, there had been a number of derailments, either due to passengers leaning out or being forced out of balance under the influence of the curve. It was almost always the last vehicle in the train that left the rails, inevitably towards the outside of the curve. Fortunately, nobody suffered anything worse than the odd bruise and shaking and a severe loss of dignity.

The problem was tackled at the end of 1973 when the bank on the Down side was cut right back almost to the boundary fence. This permitted the Up road to be moved across into the alignment previously occupied by the Down line while that track was slewed right over, close to the newly cut bank. So, from being a straight piece of track between two rather sharp curves the whole section is now gently curved throughout. In addition, the Up line received a degree of superelevation.

The second realignment directly affected the revised Phillips Bridge layout. It was found that although the long, sweeping curve of the trailing crossover looked very pleasing, and provided an excellent ride, it did present some problems, notably for trains that did not pass through it. This was due to the points having their straight sections set into the middle of curves. At speed, the sudden lurches that characterised the change from curved to straight track and back again were, at best, uncomfortable and, at worst, dangerous. There was also the secondary problem posed by the long and heavily-used Up line block through The Copse. Capacity could be increased if this was broken into two by compressing the area of the junction and crossover and installing another signal in the lengthened section thus created. So the existing crossover was taken out during November 1976 together with the point at the foot of the Spur and a new alignment surveyed. Instead of curving in gently to join the Up road almost opposite the site of the old signalbox the Spur has been shortened to make its junction some 10m above the foot of Hardwick Bank, while the crossover itself is sprung from the point where the curved track in the Up line becomes straight. The result is that tangent track has been eliminated entirely from the long curve of the Up road though there remained, for some years more, the short straight section of the point in the Down line at the Down end of the crossover.

Trackwork in Hardwick station and yard saw a number of changes. One of the sidings in the small Up side yard was extended through to join the locomotive runround road, giving an alternative route out of the headshunt into No 4 platform. Some further alterations to the yard layout followed the easing of the very tight curve on the runround road itself and a revamping of the headshunt release arrangements into a more logical configuration to afford them better protection by the signalling

there. Further development included a realigning of the pointwork in the Hardwick Central station 'throat' to allow the lengthening of platform 3 to accommodate the six-car 'Gladesman' without obstructing the passenger foot crossing at the turntable end or having the engines standing beyond the starter signal. It also permitted a slight increase in the length of platform 4. These works were ready for the 1983 season.

At the end of 1974 a 10¼" gauge siding was taken off the loco runround, from the Down end of the section behind the carriage shed, to a concrete-section garage used to store equipment for Ian Allan's commercial railways. The track up to the point of deviation had to be dual-gauge of course but the 10¼" gauge diverged at a 'blind' point which had no blades, separating stock into the proper roads by means of check rails. Following the running down of the commercial railway company the shed was handed over to the GCR; three roads were installed for the storage of the larger items of goods stock displaced from the carriage shed by the increasing number of coaches. The 10¼" line to the shed was regauged and the 'blind' point rebuilt into a normal 7¼" gauge hand worked one while the third rail behind the carriage shed was recovered for further use elsewhere. Many of the lighter, four-wheel wagons are accommodated in the old carriage shed on a raised track supported by frames fabricated from 37mm (1¹/₂") diameter piping. These frames are set through the dividing wall between the carriage and engine sheds, being mirrored in the latter where they carry shelving.

The deteriorating condition of the barn beyond the car-park required its demolition and meant that the mains water supply to the standpipe in it was cut off in late-1979. It had generally proved impossible to run a weekly summer service without making use of this facility on occasions and so an independent mains supply became an urgent necessity. Following negotiations with the Water Authority this was laid in, requiring the digging out and lining in brick of a manhole to the principal stop cock and a considerable amount of trenching for the pipe runs within the Railway's perimeter. For convenience, the standpipe in the passenger circulating area has been retained and is coupled up to the mains supply by a branch from the manhole.

Modifications to the water piping around the storage tank resulted in the water heater and tap supply in the loco shed being transferred to the mains while the tank itself could be filled from that source as well as off the engine shed roof. The latter remained the principal source for some years before being discarded in favour of the mains supply only to the water cranes.

This change resulted from an increasing demand as traffic levels grew for which the tank's storage capacity proved insufficient. Additionally, water tended to stagnate within the tank when the level was low. Loss of soft water, however, means more frequent attention has to be paid to boilers to counteract scale build-up.

Because the Railway possesses a battery-powered locomotive a powerful charger, custom-built for the job, is provided. The 'diesel' shunter, with its electric starter run off a standard car-battery in the riding truck, has its own small charger. Time switches ensure charging can be carried out without staff having to be available to supervise it and that batteries are 'full' whenever locos are required for service.

Steam-raising was performed with the help of three or four small, electrically-powered compressors feeding draught-inducing extension chimneys or, in some cases, the engine's blower itself through small-bore flexible hoses. But the 1982 season saw the introduction of a piped system from a single compressor. Another unit with a larger pump and greater holding capacity replaced it in 1985.

This compressor is fitted with a pressure switch which automatically cuts out the motor at 100psi and cuts it back in again when reservoir pressure falls below 70psi. Mounted at the West end of the shed it is convenient to the outlet points above the exit doors on all the loco shed roads; there is another outlet on the compressor itself. These outlets have variable pressure valves fitted to provide the most suitable draughting for each engine and to allow the compressor to work well within its capacity.

One of the four Cromar White points acquired from another private railway in 1981 replaced a life-expired steel point at the convergence of the crossover with the Down Main at Phillips Bridge Junction in 1982. This provided a smoother line because of its larger-radius turnout.

The Permanent Way Superintendent oversees a weed-killing programme in which all running lines and their verges are treated at least once each season. A scheme for blanketing the trackbed with black polythene sheeting to prevent weed growth and ballast loss was first tried experimentally in 1982 over Piggery Summit. But problems with drainage curtailed further applications. In any event, the availability of more effective weedkiller in recent years would have rendered it obsolete.

Above: Three long-serving GCR stalwarts, SR Class 'S15' 4-6-0 No.837, LMS Class '6P' 4-6-0 No.6100, *'Royal Scot'* and NER Class 'R1' 4-4-0 No.1239 parade in *echelon* outside the newly completed loco depot at Hardwick Central in March 1970.

Right: LMS Class '6P' 4-6-0 No.6100 *'Royal Scot'*, having passed anti-clockwise around the Everglades Loop rejoins the single line to Phillips Bridge at Fork Junction in 1970. Track to form the Up Line lies to the left.

Below: Eureka arrives at Hardwick in 1969 with a train of Liversage coaches. The incipient Down Line ends at buffer-stops by the gate.

The availability of space in the erstwhile 10¼″ gauge shed permitted an improvement to the passenger facilities at Hardwick Central. Removal to it of much of the material stored in one of the two containers and that container's conversion after cleaning out into a booking office and Sales unit allowed demolition of the small wooden hut on no 1 platform that had previously been used for this purpose. (That structure itself was secondhand, being part of the original signalbox at Phillips Bridge.) The space between the containers was cleared and roofed while the containers themselves underwent a much needed repaint. The area in front of them had some landscaping done too, making access to the new booking office window less hazardous. At the same time, a 'one-way' pedestrian system was initiated by clearance of the undergrowth alongside and behind the containers and the laying down of a 'hoggin' path. Passengers who had completed their ride left the platforms by this route to regain the station concourse; as the viewing area behind the turntable was accessible from it, they had the opportunity to linger there if they wished. Shrubs and perennials have been planted around the concourse to improve the area in general while many specimen trees and shrubs have replaced those felled due to their condition, or been put in to assist earthwork stabilisation or simply as screening. Natural recolonisation by native specimens of areas stripped of turf or skimmed for spoil has not been discouraged, while a selection of young trees parades alongside the branch. Work of this kind reflects both an increasing awareness of the potential attractiveness of the Railway's surroundings as a whole, and a conscious effort to improve and develop them when and where possible.

There was a very real possibility during the mid-70s that the route of the M25 Motorway, then at the planning stage, would take at least a slice, and perhaps a lot more out of the Railway's site, a Damoclesion sword overhanging all the progress made up to and throughout that period. Fortunately, its line was finally established further to the East, roughly parallel to and within 80m of the branch terminus at Cockcrow Hill. As the ground between is quite open, each is plainly visible from the other. The reactions of car drivers and their passengers who are not 'in the know' suddenly catching a glimpse of a train trundling solemnly over the level crossing or pounding away from the station are a constant source of amusement on the Railway side of the fence.

Construction of the motorway, however, caused problems. As it is on embankment for most of its length in the vicinity, the engineers had to divert and provide numerous culverts for the drainage ditches which criss-cross the area and eventually find their way into the Thames. These works altered the whole pattern of drainage in all the nearby fields, including those of the GCR, so much so that the level of water in the stream through the south-eastern corner dropped by more than half a metre overnight. It became apparent as time passed that this was due to a drastic change in the level of the water table, presumably caused by the excavation of material to construct the embankment. The result was that many streams and ditches changed their character radically; in the case of those at the West end of the Railway, for example, the direction of flow was reversed so that drainage water ran into the pond at Everglades. No amount of tinkering seemed to have the desired effect of re-establishing the status quo. There was nothing for it but to set up a whole new programme of drainage work to counteract the problem, which involved digging out some 120m of ditching through the middle of the site to feed water into the stream. The ditch had to be over two metres deep in places to maintain the flow. The work, all done by hand, was spread over three seasons and completely drained Pig Pond at last.

Two new bridges, of ex-BR timber sleepers, were built over the ditch in March 1982. One of these replaced the original culvert under the Jungle line while the other carries Meadowside.

During March 1983, the engine and carriage sheds were extended by five metres. An enginemen's lobby and oil store occupied the new space in the loco shed, while the extension provided additional accommodation in the carriage shed for the passenger stock fleet, which had had to be stacked from some seasons to get it all under cover. When the new carriage shed opened in 1989 this extension was handed over to the Permanent Way department for track building and repair.

The public had always been very indulgent about the lack of cover provided for them in wet weather. A long overdue move to remedy this was undertaken in mid-April 1985 with the erection of two platform canopies at Hardwick Central. One is on the island platform, nos 2 and 3, the other covers platform 1, providing shelter for people queuing for trains. At present, platform 4 remains open to the elements.

A more pressing need showed up in 1984. Repair and maintenance of signalling equipment at Everglades Junction and, in particular, the expeditious tracing of faults had become increasingly difficult. This was because the power signalling installation, as it spread through the Everglades control area, was served by piecemeal additions to the wiring in the signalbox. (The building itself was long overdue for refurbishment that could not properly be done with equipment in situ.) In these circumstances, the S&T Engineer considered that satisfactory operation during 1985 could not be assured.

The frame from South Croydon Junction box, made redundant on commissioning of the Three Bridges control centre, had been purchased in 1984 with a view to replacing Everglades box during 1985/6. But the Committee decided to bring construction forward a year in the light of the S&T Engineer's fears.

A site to the West of the existing box was cleared and levelled during November 1984, the spoil dug out of the ridge there being deposited along the embankment towards Piggery Summit. A concrete foundation raft of some 3.7m by 3m was laid down in early December.

It was necessary to build the box around the frame, but when the latter had been positioned construction work was brought to an abrupt halt by freezing weather during the first eight weeks of the new year. The bitter cold did not deter the S&T staff, however. Protected from the worst of the elements by a tarpaulin slung over the frame they continued the tedious task of wiring up. This also included running cables to the old box — now the relay room — and out to the points which, under the new scheme, are equipped for electrical instead of mechanical operation.

The five new point motors had been constructed early in the year but could not be placed in position nor wired up until the weather relented. By 25 March, however, the work was complete, though trenching the cables and encasing them in 110mm plastic piping was not finally finished until May.

The great mass of cabling snaking its way between the new box and the old, which had been stripped of its frame as soon as the 1984 season closed to make way for new wiring looms and relay racks, was cocooned and buried by the end of February. The weather had relented enough by then for construction work on the new box to resume.

The walls with their steel-frame windows were complete by 24 March but the hipped roof and ancillary items like fascia boards and guttering had not been finished when the 1985 season opened on 5 May.

Below: Surrounded by building materials the Everglades Junction signal frame stands in the open with the temporary track diagram above it. Throughout the 1970 season block and token instruments were temporarily wired up to permit operation of the line. The box was built around the frame in the Spring of 1971.

CONSOLIDATION: (ii): 1986 Onwards

The design of the new Everglades signalbox had coincided with the appointment of an Environmental Officer on the Committee. His remit primarily concerned planning and instituting a general policy of improvement to the Railway's infrastructure and surroundings. The object was to provide a more integrated and cohesive image and embraced everything from colour schemes to major developments. The finish of the tunnel portals and the reconstruction of Hardwick signalbox, on much the same lines and in the same materials as the one at Everglades, provided evidence of this policy being practised.

The original Hardwick box comprised a block-built shed with a corrugated asbestos sheet roof that sloped from one end of the building to the other. From November 1986, as the first stage in a four-year redevelopment of the Hardwick area, the front and end walls of the box were demolished and a further slice of soil removed to permit extension at the western end. The new box, of block and brick construction, arose around the lever frame, to which the eight ex-Phillips Bridge levers were added temporarily. It featured small-pane windows as at Everglades and a ridge roof with slate covering.

Delay in the delivery of the window frames meant a flurry of activity during April though the box was ready for use when the 1987 season opened. The dogs' tooth bargeboards, were not in place until the end of June.

The steady growth of traffic, and the rise in the number of engines required each Sunday to cope with it, showed the need for more space for loco steaming and preparation. This was met by extending the loco shed pits under the third line from the shed itself and the adjoining one from the carriage shed. Under the long-term plan this shed would

become part of the loco depot, the carriages being housed in a new building elsewhere in the compound.

It took some six weeks to complete excavation of the extension, spoil being railed out to repair slippage on The Causeway and Hardwick Bank. As on the original pit roads, track is bolted to the top surface of the spanning girders, the RSJs on the extension being deep enough to cross the gap without any intermediate support. This is a distinct advantage over the older lines when unimpeded access beneath an engine is needed. The girders were set in place at the end of March, after the extended concrete floor and the brick retaining walls around the pit were completed. Track outside the carriage shed was rearranged to provide only three roads to the turntable so as to get adequate clearance within the pit, though a point in the shed itself permitted the retention of four roads there.

During 1987 new points were designed for a revised Hardwick layout. The original formation used pointwork recovered from Greywood and showed all too clearly how alignments had been dictated by point configuration rather than vice-versa.

As soon as the 1987 season had come to a close the old LNWR frames were disconnected and removed from Hardwick box to be replaced by 23 levers from the Westinghouse 'L' frame out of Crewe South Junction box. The prospective conversion of signalling at Hardwick to power operation made this change necessary.

Semaphores were retained, an electro-magnetic mechanism being fitted to each arm. The Everglades system of DC split-field motors for point operation had proved very successful and was adopted for the Hardwick layout too.

It had been decided to enhance flexibility of operation by extending all four platforms to accommodate six-car trains. This meant all the starting signals had to be moved and required the whole of the station throat to be compressed, a change taken into account in designing the new pointwork.

The new layout included a 'Dock Road' on the opposite face of the outer end of platform 4, to hold a set of stock ready for immediate use. This line was served off the Through siding and its installation saw the removal of the last of the Up sidings alongside the latter. Plain track was shifted into the new alignments when the platform extensions were complete; the points were laid in and wired up as soon as they became available.

Work on a new ballast delivery and storage area began in November 1987. Its purpose was to do away with the double-handling the existing arrangement entailed, restrict wastage and increase storage capacity. It

Below: The Down end starting signals at Everglades Junction in 1974, the left-hand arm of the Down Main starter bracket authorised a movement to the Spur line. The signalbox in the background is now the relay room.

is situated on the Down side, beyond the compound, and is capable of storing up to 20 tons of ballast.

The bank alongside the Down Main was cut back to the vertical for some five metres and excavated down to about 30cms below ambient ground level, the excavations being filled with compacted hardcore and a 15cm thick concrete raft. A girder-supported track, similar in construction to those over the loco pit, was erected in March 1988, after the brick retaining walls had been built and backfilled. Apart from the ease of unloading, the arrangement allows ballast to be shovelled off a hard even surface and any overflow from wagons to fall back into the pit.

Access to the siding is by a facing point in the Down Main so the line was often used as an engine refuge during shunting moves. A loco delivery track is provided off the ballast siding, a hinged bridge spanning the gap to motor vehicle or trailer. The pit area came into use in April 1988. From 1994, the siding was locked out of use following the transition of its point motor to the Jubilee Line divergence.

The dirt track in the car-park, alongside the fence of the compound, was resurfaced in May 1988 with compacted hoggin to cater for the heavy trucks delivering ballast to the new pit.

The GCR formed one of the venues for the 'Woking 150' celebrations on 29 and 30 May 1988. Well over 1,000 visitors were carried each day, despite some poor weather, and the Railway featured prominently in the video made of the event.

Another 150th Anniversary was celebrated in July, that of 'Mail by Rail', marked by a 'Royal Mail Steam Day' on which some 2000 Post Office staff and their families were entertained. The Railway's car-park was taken over by sideshows, amusements, exhibits and displays; a local farmer permitted parking near Cockcrow Hill in a field off the main Chertsey-Woking road. This necessitated operation, for the first hour or so before 'normal' service, of a continuous shuttle of double-headed six-car trains to bring visitors to Hardwick Central. The Railway retains a memento of the event in the shape of a superb Post Office mail sorting van complete with pick-up apparatus.

A more private celebration took place in September to mark the 75th 'birthday' of the railway's oldest locomotive, the NER 'R1' class 4-4-0. A very relaxed atmosphere, with invited guests, provided a great contrast to the usual state of affairs when the line is open to the public.

Outline schemes for a new carriage shed were drawn up during that summer since this formed the major work to be undertaken the 1988/9 winter. The favoured site had been that now occupied by the ballast pit but an area on the other side of the line was ultimately chosen, which also provided space for a proper coaling stage alongside the runround.

The garage that first held 10¼" gauge stock and then GCR freight vehicles had been dismantled and sold in 1986 leaving a suitable, level site, but only if the sidings in it made connections at the eastern rather than western end as had been the case before. This change demanded an extension of the loco headshunt beyond the boundary fence and the installation of a gate in place of the chain-link.

From the options drawn up, the design ultimately adopted was for a 14.5m long, five-road building providing accommodation for 30 'standard' coaches. It is of the usual block and brick construction under a slated ridge roof crowned by a three-faced clock tower. Frosty weather delayed progress after the foundations had been poured before the turn of the year and this delay was reflected by the building still being incomplete when the 1989 season opened in May. Indeed, some of the ridge tiles were not added until the following winter.

Initially, the shed contained three roads. These fed into the loco headshunt extension, which parallels the Up Main for some 20m beyond the compound boundary. The dead-end siding that had served the Goods Shed was later extended behind the new shed to join up with the headshunt, so forming a by-pass road for engines that did not need a full service between turns. The other two lines in the shed diverged off this. These arrangements, and a water tank alongside the by-pass line, became available in March 1990. From the start of that season, shunting stock from the station to the carriage shed was controlled by new shunt signals below the starters at Hardwick. Previously, such movements into the headshunt had been prohibited.

That year also marked the total changeover to the mains water supply, which required a new manhole with stopcocks to be provided by the loco shed and complete renewal of the hoses to all the various outlets.

Elsewhere in Hardwick the booking office from London Underground's Ravenscourt Park station arrived in December 1988. This replaced the ancient and leaky container that had served the purpose for many years. Work had been going on during the summer to improve the viewing

area behind the turntable, removal of the containers permitting this to continue during the 1988/9 winter and the one following.

The most urgent need, however, was to roof the new booking office, which had been recovered from the interior of the booking hall, and provide it with bargeboards like those on the signalbox.

Work on the viewing area involved building a brick retaining wall from the turntable to the exit gate and raising, levelling and paving the area behind it. This area is reached by a ramp, making it accessible to wheelchair users, and is stoutly fenced and provided with seats. The circulating area around the booking office was paved too, improving both safety and appearance. These facilities were available from the start of the 1990 season.

Another viewing area came into use at that time as an adjunct to a new tea room beside the line outside Hardwick Central station. Selling refreshments has proved to be a very useful source of revenue, all profits being ploughed back into the Railway.

Two major works of quite different character occupied the 1990/1 winter. The first involved the provision of a separate line from Bishops Culvert to Everglades Junction for use by Up Branch trains. The build-up of traffic had stretched the capacity of the Down Main between these points, even at only moderately busy times. Shortening and increasing the number of sections had had little effect beyond the short term.

Pegging out the new line and the required deviations to Up and Down Main lines took place in July 1990; widening The Causeway began as soon as the new alignments were agreed upon. Grubbing out the massive roots of the Oak tree felled by lightning in 1982 became one of the first tasks; the Down Main now passes right over the spot. Spoil for The Causeway came from the inner face of the cutting around Piggery Summit though some went down to widen the bank on the approach to Everglades through the old Pig Pond. With additional pipework being needed in the culvert here, the opportunity was taken to reconstruct it entirely with larger-diameter piping.

The widened trackbed was finished by the end of the year, permitting the Up Main line to be slewed over into its new alignment. Under the scheme, the Down Main became the Up Branch; by mid-February, the new Down Main track, together with a Down Main-Down Loop crossover at Everglades, had been laid in and bonded to allow track-circuiting to be tested before ballasting. Two months later the line was ready for service.

The second major project for that winter concerned a complete rewiring of Everglades area's signalling and replacement of all power cables and equipment. The existing signalling depended largely on second-hand material obtained from BR and other sources. Much of this would not have met the safety recommendations of the new Health and Safety Executive and, in any event, most was life-expired.

Westinghouse undertook the signalling work as a joint exercise, stripping out all the old gear and starting with a 'clean sheet'. The Railway's own staff erected the new relay cabinets required for this and tackled the rewiring of the power installation, prompted by the provision of 3-phase electricity on site. Full operation had taxed the original single-phase source, the Railway being at the end of the power line and subject to distinct voltage drop.

Signalling re-equipment began in February and continued until the beginning of May, with some staff camping on site during the latter part of April. Though complete by the advertised opening day, due to some very long hours being put in, there had not been time to test the new installation fully. Reluctantly, and to the disappointment of many potential passengers, opening was delayed for one week on safety grounds for the necessary checks to be made.

One important signalling change concerned the approach to Hardwick. There had been an increasing incidence of 'run-bys' at the Inner Home gantry, which is out of a driver's line of vision until his engine rounds the curve on the approach to the Outer Home. None of these had resulted in anything of serious consequence, but a cause and solution had to be found.

The investigators came to the conclusion that drivers coming up the bank expected the Inner Home to be 'off' when the Outer Home showed 'clear' or, more particularly, if it 'cleared' as they approached it. Part of this psychological problem lay in the shortness of the section between the two signals. And there is a natural reluctance to stop a train on a steeply rising gradient if at all avoidable, since this is a very difficult place to start away from. A sense of relief at seeing the 'Outer' come off possibly left the driver concentrating more on getting his train away than looking at the 'Inner'. Moreover, in looking up at the gantry one faces directly into the sun, something that does not help the proper sighting of signals.

The problem was solved by providing a 'Warning' arm below the Outer

Home, the two working off the same lever in the frame. If the lever is pulled but the Inner Home is at 'Danger', the 'Warning' arm will clear when the train hits the approach track circuit, eliminating any doubt about the position of the Inner Home.

The 1990/1 close season saw, too, the equipping of a workshop. During the previous winter the inner-end of the concrete-section shed on the North side of the car park had been separated from the outer end by a block wall with swing double-doors for access. The floor and walls in the inner half were sealed against damp, lighting and power provision greatly improved and a programme of construction of work benches and handling frames instituted. In addition, the shop was provided with heavy lifting gear.

The result is that most of the engineering work, including major overhauls and repairs, can now be undertaken on site. Plans for the rest of the shed to be converted to workshop use are now in hand.

Cockcrow Hill and Everglades Junction were both the subject of environmental attention the following winter. At Everglades, the platforms were extended at the Down end, the Down Loop platform being widened at the same time, which involved cutting back the earth bank behind it and building a new brick retaining wall. Access to the platforms was improved and a new lattice signal gantry provided in place of the bracket put in when the area went over to power signalling. The water cranes had to be moved forward too and the Up Siding acquired a release loop.

At Cockcrow Hill, changes to the infrastructure and signalling to permit parallel working were put in hand. The engine release line became a platform road, the Up side platform being widened to form an island beneath the canopy built in August 1990. The Down platform was abolished since the road adjoining it became the loco release line under the new scheme. But track to form a new platform road went in on the Down side of this line, though it had no connections at the Up end until it was brought into operation in 1993.

It had been anticipated that the signalbox, whose roof in particular had deteriorated rapidly, would be rebuilt for 1992. But time constraints put reconstruction back a year. To some extent the nature of the rebuilding depended upon the style of lever frame to be used for the proposed power signalling installation. The fact that one had not been found to suit the Railway's requirements tipped the balance in favour of delaying rebuilding.

As it turned out, no frame became available during the subsequent year either so the rebuilt box retained the same floor area despite the fact that some diminution would almost certainly have been possible with a power frame.

As in the other two boxes, small-paned windows went into rebuilt walls under a hipped, slate roof similar to the one at Everglades, and a timber floor was provided above the cold concrete base raft. The roof ridge and bargeboards were added in June 1993 though the box had come into use at the start of that season.

Signalling alterations were confined to the changes in track use though the old Inner Home post with its theatre-type route indicator gave way to a splendid four-arm bracket. Parallel working came into operation with

the 1992 season: 1993 saw the third platform road in use and track for a freight road in place though not connected until 1994. The fence between the platform and the freight line sports some nostalgic enamel advertisements, a feature of Everglades Junction too.

The increase in usage in the workshop and the prospect of its enlargement brought into sharper focus long-standing suggestions for the provision of rail access. The scheme adopted postulated a steeply-graded spur to the workshop from a completely new line around the lower car-park field that provided a 'relief' Down road to Phillips Bridge Junction. This extension, of some 290m (960ft) brings the total track length used by passenger services to about 2380m (1.47 miles).

The routes were surveyed and pegged out in September 1992 for feasibility before a final decision was taken. In view of Health & Safety Executive recommendations, a new shed for non-steam engines was worked into the scheme, occupying an area beside the workshop. Another turntable and runround facilities were also included in the proposal together with a low-level road for materials delivery.

Once proposed levels and alignments had been finalised and approved construction began. Almost all the new line is above ambient ground level so building up the necessary embanking was put out to contract. The earthworks rose during the 1993 summer, latterly in very heavy rain. Nevertheless, they had been completed by September.

It was decided that the line should be opened officially on 9 July 1994 and be named the 'Jubilee Line.' Tracklaying began from the Phillips Bridge end and was finished by the middle of June with the installation of the point at the divergence. Final ballasting was only completed during the week preceding the line's inauguration. The artist, Terence Cuneo, performed the honours and the occasion was marked by a cavalcade of nine engines, many of them invited specially to the proceedings. The line came into immediate, though restricted, use and has already proved very popular. A level-crossing over it between the two car-parking fields will be complete for 1995.

The non-steam shed, an extended concrete-section building with four tracks, was erected in August 1993. Connection from the workshop spur is scheduled for the 1994/5 winter.

Apart from the new line, the rewiring of the Hardwick signalling system formed the major undertaking for 1993/4. A large 'portacabin' had arrived on site in December 1992; part of this is devoted to a staff 'messing' and 'clean' room whilst the rest houses the new relays.

The racks were set up and much preliminary work on the rewiring accomplished during the 1993 season. This demonstrated how much more room there would be than in the two relay cabinets then in use, making wiring changes and additions, as well as any fault tracing, much easier to manage. Removal of the cabinets also improved the sighting line from Hardwick box towards Phillips Bridge.

Though maintenance demands have to take precedence, developments of this nature are continual. Cockcrow Hill's resignalling and remodelling are still in the pipeline and the layout at Phillips Bridge is subject to some long looks and varied ideas for improvement. Such things are essential if the continued interest of staff and customers is to be maintained.

Right: The new signalbox at Everglades Junction takes shape in 1985 beside the old one, destined to become the relay room under the new signalling scheme.

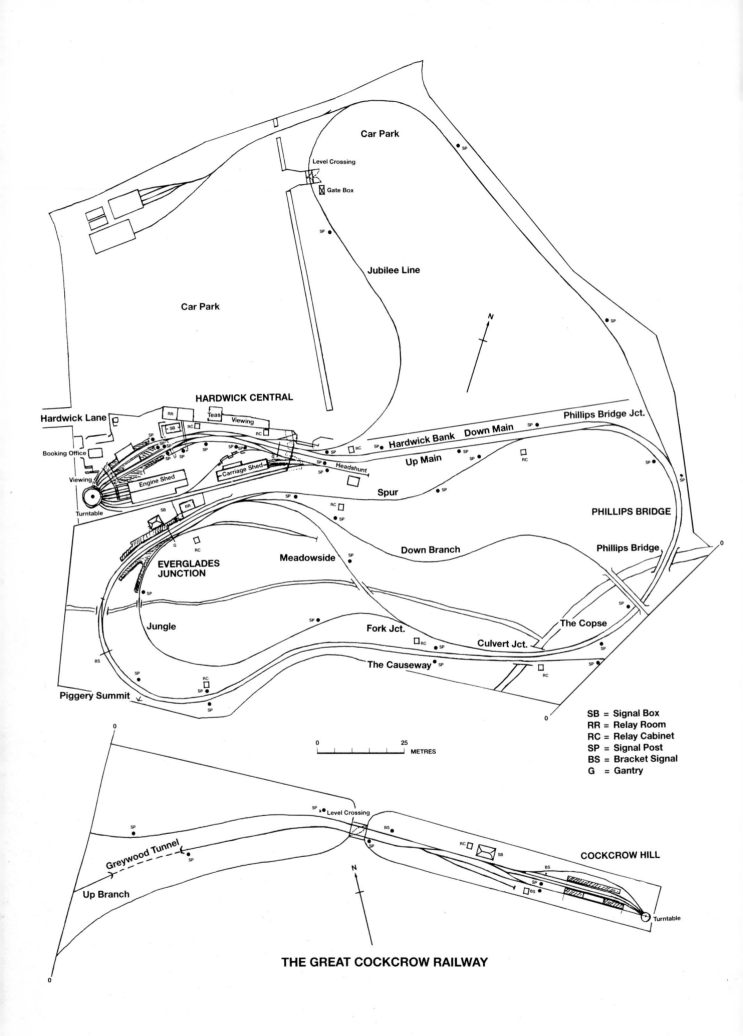

Car Park

Level Crossing

⊠ Gate Box

Jubilee Line

• SP

• SP

Car Park

↗N

• SP

HARDWICK CENTRAL

Phillips Bridge Jct.

Hardwick Lane

RR

Teas

Viewing

SB

RC

RC

Hardwick Bank   Down Main

• SP

Booking Office

SP

SP

SP

RC

• SP

• SP

Up Main

• SP

RC

• SP

Viewing

SP

SP

Carriage Shed

SP

SP

Headshunt

Spur

• SP

Engine Shed

• SP

Turntable

SB

RR

RC

• SP

PHILLIPS BRIDGE

G

RC

Down Branch

Phillips Bridge

**EVERGLADES
JUNCTION**

Meadowside

• SP

• SP

• SP

The Copse

Jungle

• SP

Fork Jct.

Culvert Jct.

• SP

• SP

BS

RC

• SP

• SP

Piggery Summit

RC

The Causeway • SP

RC

• SP

SP

SP

SB = Signal Box
RR = Relay Room
RC = Relay Cabinet
SP = Signal Post
BS = Bracket Signal
G = Gantry

0 ———————— 25
METRES

0

SP • Level Crossing

• SP

BS

Greywood Tunnel

• SP

RC

SB

BS

COCKCROW HILL

↑N

SP

Up Branch

BS

⊕ Turntable

0

THE GREAT COCKCROW RAILWAY

0

SIGNALLING & OPERATING

Realistic operation has been a feature of the GCR since early days at Greywood, the use of signals and proper signalling procedure ensuring the continued safety of passengers and smooth running of the Railway. Before going into detail it may be appropriate to describe briefly the procedure employed on the prototype, which forms the basis of GCR operations.

The 'main' or 'running' lines — as opposed to 'siding' lines — are divided into sections. These sections are usually termed 'block sections' or just 'blocks', each 'block' being controlled from a signalbox. Block length is determined by a number of factors including the complications of the trackwork within it and the density of the service over it. The trains are controlled within each block by signals and passed from block to block or, in other words, from signalman to signalman, by use of 'Block instruments', (see fig i). Each running line has an instrument for its exclusive use so a signalman having just one 'Up' line and one 'Down' line will have two block instruments in his box; a busy box with, say, four running lines will have four instruments and so on. To see how the system operates let us take one of a pair of running lines (see fig ii), and suppose that the signalman in box X has a train on his block ready to proceed on to block Y. He will 'Call attention' by 'stroking' — that is, depressing, — once, the plunger (a in fig i) on his block instrument for that line, which rings once the single-beat bell on the appropriate instrument in signal-box Y. Signalman Y will indicate he is ready with one stroke on the plunger of his instrument giving a single beat on the signal box X bell (d). Signalman X will then 'offer' the train, describing its type by a recognisable code, for example, 3 beats — pause — 1 beat, 'ordinary passenger train.' If block Y is clear, signalman Y will repeat the code back to signalman X to indicate he can 'accept' the train and will move the handle (b) on his instrument so that the needle (c) indicates 'Line Clear.' This indication is repeated on the instrument in signalbox X by the upper needle (e). Seeing this 'Line Clear' indication, Signalman X will pull off the appropriate signals and when the train passes into block Y, he will advise Signalman Y by two strokes — the 'Train entering section' signal — which will be acknowledged by the usual repetition and by movement of the handle (b) on the signalbox Y block instrument so the needle shows 'Train on line.' As before, this indication is repeated by the needle (e) in signalbox X so that both signalmen are aware that there is a train 'on the block' between them. Signalman Y now assumes the role previously played by Signalman X, offering the train forward to Signalman Z and, if it is accepted, pulling

off his signals to allow it to proceed forward. Once it is clear of his section, Signalman Y will call Signalman X's attention and then send him the code 2 beats — pause — 1 beat, 'Train out of section', and return his instrument to the 'Line Blocked' position so that all is ready to be repeated when the next train comes along.

It will be seen from fig iii that each signalman is placed at the end of the block under his control; this applies to lines for both directions thus:-

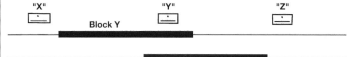

He is, therefore, in a position to ensure that the block section of track for which he is responsible is clear before he accepts another train into it. Although this description of procedure is very basic, the many variations, both as regards instrumentation and operation, all conform to the principle of 'Block Signalling' as illustrated here.*

As we saw in Chapter 1 control at Greywood, with the exception of the small terminus at Greywood North, was vested in one centrally-placed signalbox. But the extended nature of the new GCR made similar operation with semaphore signalling, which prevailed at the time, impossible. It was decided at the outset that three signalboxes would be required, at Hardwick Central, Phillips Bridge and Everglades, and they were constructed and in operation by 1970. Signalling was entirely semaphore except for a small colour-light installation in the remote area of The Causeway using items recovered from Greywood North. Block instruments were installed in all three boxes while movements over the Spur were governed by Tyer's No: 12A type single-line token instruments in Phillips Bridge and Everglades boxes. These two boxes became very demanding to work as traffic increased; signalmen at Phillips Bridge got used to all three block bells ringing at once! In these circumstances, and realising that traffic was likely to go on increasing as the Railway became better known, it was decided, in conjunction with the track changes made in 1973, to close Phillips Bridge box and install colour-light signals in its area to be controlled from a panel in Everglades box. The effects of this change were two-fold. Firstly, by reverting to Greywood's example of a central signalling position better use could be made of available manpower and, secondly, operation of the line would, it was felt, become more efficient.

In addition this marked the beginning of a general changeover to colour-light signalling, a move regretted by many of the staff but recognised as being necessary if the most efficient use was to be made of the revised layout while maintaining the required high standard of safety. So the colour-lights came in and with them the first large-scale application of track-circuiting to add to the small installation along The Causeway.

To those wishing to explore further the intricacies of signalling practice the book British Railway Signalling, by Geoffrey Kichenside and Alan Williams, published by Ian Allan, is recommended.

Below: A Signalman's eye view of Everglades Junction box in 1993. The vintage LNWR block instrument at the left hand end of the block shelf contrasts with the computerised train describer to the right. Red painted levers operate signals, black ones points, white levers are spares.

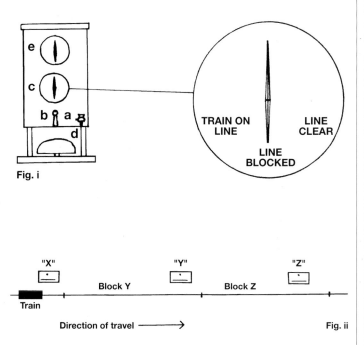

39

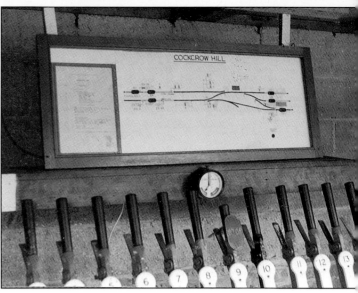

Above: The interior of Hardwick Central signalbox. The Westinghouse 'L' type frame is ex-Crewe South Junction, and there is plenty of 'spit and polish' on the instruments above it.

Above right: The signalbox diagram shows the very simple layout at Cockcrow Hill in 1992. The tops of the full-size ex-Midland Railway levers are visible. A third platform line has been commissioned since.

Further extensions were planned but had to be held over as the generator could not have coped with the additional load.

The arrival of mains power at the end of 1973, permitted extension of power signalling into the Everglades area. By stages, all the Main line outside the immediate environs of Hardwick Central, including the few remaining semaphores, was converted between 1975 and 1979.

The box that comes first to visitors' attention is the one at Hardwick Central. Being immediately adjacent to the circulating area the signalman there is under almost constant surveillance. It contains a Westinghouse 'L' frame of 23 levers, ex-Crewe South, that came into use in 1988.

The floor of the box is sunk some 50cm below rail level, which permitted the original mechanical connections to points and signals, worked by a LNWR two-tier frame of 19 miniature levers, to go out through the front wall.

The block shelf above the frame supports the block instrument to Everglades Junction and an illuminated diagram of the station — a feature of all three signal boxes — showing the relative positions of all signals under the box's control. The diagram is termed 'illuminated' because it keeps the signalman informed of line occupancy within his area, 'closed' track circuits 'illuminating' two lights in the appropriate track section on the diagram. Track-circuits on the Up Main as far out as Phillips Bridge Junction are shown on the diagram, partly as a safety measure and partly to keep the signalman appraised of traffic movements immediately beyond his vision. This arrangement was introduced in 1980 and is a considerable help when planning light-engine or shunting moves within the station which might otherwise perhaps check or stop an incoming service.

Of the eight points in the layout in mechanical signalling days, five were operated by rodding while the other three and all 13 semaphore signals were worked by wire pulling against a return spring. This system, if set up properly, works very well over distances up to about 50m. Signals are both upper- and lower-quadrant types to ⅛th scale, the former based on BR practice, the latter of Great Central design from Greywood. Various shunt signals are also in evidence.

Two theatre-type route indicators operate in conjunction with the headshunt release signal to advise the driver which platform he is destined for. Clearance of the signal also sets ringing a shunt bell which ceases its cacophony when the engine clears the headshunt track-circuit.

The gantry on which the headshunt release signal is mounted also carries the four Up Inner Homes authorising entry to the platforms. It featured a banner repeater for the Down Advanced Starting signal but that was superseded by the junction signals for the Down Main/Down Loop (Jubilee Line) divergence when that came into operation in 1994. The gantry came into use in 1973 in place of the original 4-arm bracket.

One signal not operated by the Hardwick signalman but visible from his box is the Phillips Bridge Down Distant. This is mounted beneath the Hardwick Advanced Starter and is controlled by clearance of the colour-light signal at the foot of Hardwick Bank. However, as in full-size practice, where a 'stop' signal and a 'distant' signal are on the same post, the latter is worked by a slotted arrangement to ensure it cannot clear before the starter above it does so, and will return to 'caution' when the starter returns to 'danger'.

Moving down Hardwick Bank, the next signalbox the visitor in early days would have passed was Phillips Bridge. It was situated at the start of the curve beyond the present Phillips Bridge Junction though no trace of it now remains except the concrete base hidden beneath the undergrowth. This box was arguably the busiest of the original three yet it only had eight levers in its frame, also ex-LNWR as at Hardwick. Apart from controlling the signals in its immediate vicinity the box also worked the point at the top of Hardwick Bank where the original Spur led off to Everglades Junction from the Up Main. This was a very long 'pull' requiring careful adjustment of the operating wire and return springs in view of the relatively short travel of the miniature levers.

Although the Down line was signalled so that trains from Hardwick as well as those off the Spur could enter the Down Loop, they never did so after the second track on the Polish Corridor came into full use in 1970. The track changes of 1973 wholly altered the layout in this area and made points, signals and box redundant. The box contained two block instruments, one each for the Up and Down lines, plus the single-line token instrument to control the Spur interlocked with a similar machine at Everglades. It was generally agreed that the signalman here needed to be agile in both mind and body. Much of his afternoon was spent galloping up and down the entrance steps to hand out or collect the single-line token, often with a block bell ringing a peremptory summons through the open window! There were mixed feelings of relief and regret when this box closed its door for the last time and its responsibilities were assumed by Everglades. The building lingered for some years housing the relays required to operate the new signalling; when these had been moved to the relay cabinet at the junction it was re-erected at Cockcrow Hill during the spring of 1982 to provide shelter in inclement weather for passengers at that exposed terminus!

With the transfer of signalling responsibility from Phillips Bridge, Everglades became the 'nerve centre' of the Railway. As at Hardwick, the frame in the original box was of miniature levers but of a Westinghouse Brake & Signal Company's type, containing eighteen levers in three groups of six in a straight line. There was also an ex-South Eastern Railway 'fog frame' of two levers to operate the mechanical points at the extreme ends of the station layout. Unlike Hardwick the floor of this box was raised well above rail level so that the 'below-floor' interlocking mechanism and the connections to the operating wires outside could be accommodated in a pit at the front of the box. (The interlocking on the LNWR frame at Hardwick, incidentally, was housed on the signalman's side of the frame, nicely placed to bark the shins of the unwary!) The block shelf supported a LNWR block instrument and the illuminated diagram together with the 'panel' controlling the Phillips Bridge area, which had the operating switches set into its face on a diagrammatic representation of the layout.

Right: New power cables are hauled into position as the Everglades rewiring programme progresses in the 1990/1 winter.

In the last year or two before colour light signalling was fully installed, the box became very demanding, both mentally — which, to a marked degree, it still is — and physically. The miniature levers required strong yet dextrous fingers to take up the longer pulls, which invariably had the most powerful return springs. On a practical note, the longest pulls round the curve to the Everglades Down Distants were very tricky to set up properly and even more difficult to maintain, particularly as temperature changes played havoc with the springing adjustment. Similar adjustment problems were found on other long pulls. There was also the question of adequately signalling the branch and the new connections to it from the Everglades end: colour-lights seemed the only answer if some extremely difficult and complicated mechanical interlocking in the frame was to be avoided. Despite the more involved track layout occasioned by the Branch, the number of levers in use in the miniature frame of this box came down from seventeen under the mechanical system to only 13 when the initial electric signalling installation was complete.

From 1978, when the branch opened, until doubling in 1984 the box housed a Tyer's single-line token instrument electrically interlocked with a similar instrument at Cockcrow Hill. The principle under which the system works is quite simple. Only one token can be withdrawn at a time, an operation requiring the co-operation of both signalmen, and both instruments remain locked until that token is replaced. Coupled with this is the rule that no driver can run his train on to the single line unless he is in possession of a token. Those used on the GCR took the form of a key though there are many variations, depending on the system

in use. However, the basic principle remains the same.

The new box, commissioned at the opening of the 1985 season on 5 May, has the complete Westinghouse frame of 31 miniature levers from South Croydon. Fortunately it was purchased with all the electrical slide connection apparatus, which is housed in a cabinet behind the frame itself, as well as signal and point repeaters mounted immediately above the relevant levers. The block instrument and illuminated diagram were transferred from the old box though several changes had to be made to the latter to reflect the increase in the number of track circuits in the new scheme as well as the wholesale renumbering of points and signals. (The separate panel which controlled the Phillips Bridge area was, of course, made redundant.)

Unlike Hardwick, where all the area controlled is in view of the signalman, the Everglades man, or rather, men since the box generally needs a staff of two on duty, are very dependent on the illuminated diagram for information as they can only see some 10% of their area. It shows all the Railway from a point immediately outside the compound gates at Hardwick to the Everglades side of the viaduct on the Down Branch and the level crossing on the Up, which may give some idea to the reader of the extent and complexity of the signalmens' task. On the more heavily used sections headways may be as little as ½ minute, illustrating just how essential power signalling and track-circuiting have become for the signalmen's peace of mind.

To help further, the box is equipped with a 4-character train describer which codes each train according to destination and allocates it a sequential number for identification purposes. The screen mimics the

Above: Steve Clark of Westinghouse is among the spaghetti of wiring in the Everglades Junction relay room in 1992.

Right: GCR signal technician Graham Hill works on the wiring in the Fork Junction relay cabinet in 1991

Above: Hardwick Central platform No.4 starting signals; the ringed arm permits movement into the Up Through siding.

layout, the description moving from section to section as the train progresses, precisely as in full size practice. The position and type of each colour-light signal on the layout and the density of traffic over the particular section of track signalled decide which of two-, three- or four-aspects the colour light 'head' should be. All signals return to 'danger' when a train passes them into the next track-circuit section: nine signals are wholly automatic. The colour-light signal heads are not permanently attached to the posts — or the gantries in the case of the Everglades Junction Down Homes and Starters — and it is the practice to remove them for safe, undercover storage at the end of each operating session and remount them again at the beginning of the next. Indeed the first and last services run each day are the Signals Trains. Connections to the power source on each post are made with multi-pin plugs.

Semaphore signals outside the secure compound area at Hardwick are also removable, though in these cases the whole post lifts out of a square section steel tube sunk into the ground. There were four electrically worked semaphores powered by redundant BR 110v shunt-signal motors acquired from 1979. They were the Distant below the Hardwick Advanced Starter, and Distant and Home signals governing Up movements on the Spur towards Everglades Junction. The first of these was provided with a post-mounted solenoid when the Hardwick

installation was electrified in 1987 but the others remained a semaphore oasis in Everglades' control area until the 1993 season when they, too, were superseded by colour-lights.

Five powered points are worked off the Everglades frame; four are in the layout there and the fifth at the foot of the Spur at its junction with the Up Main. This point was the only one power-operated from the old box. The first mechanism installed consisted of a small motor attached by a universal coupling to a threaded shaft. A bracket with a threaded block at its upper end hanging from this shaft was coupled to an extension of the point blade tie-bar through a sliding locking arrangement. When the motor was energised it turned the shaft, moving the block along it to change the point. Despite the coarseness of the thread point-changing took several seconds but more seriously the motor proved to be underpowered. Nevertheless, it lasted for three seasons. From 1977 a new system was installed built around a DC split-field motor of good power and extreme reliability with a direct drive to the point and locking mechanism. This performed very well, the only weakness being the substantial power input required to work it. The opportunity was taken to replace it with a new 'standard' mechanism like those fitted when the existing mechanical points were changed over to power operation. The drive in these comes from a windscreen wiper motor fitted with an adjustable eccentric to allow for variations in point blade movement, that converts rotary action into linear motion. The drive is designed, too, to lock and 'detect' point blades in the 'closed' position at the conclusion of point changing. 'Spring' points are also detected to prove track circuits and confirm to the signalmen that the blades have closed properly after the passage of trains in the trailing direction. From 1988 the point giving access to the Up Siding was mechanically-worked by a ground frame released from the signalbox. Power operation from the main frame, together with new entry and exit signals, is planned for 1995.

With the proliferation of control relays — and the cabinets housing them form a prominent feature at stations and junctions — safety and information systems can be built in which would have been difficult, if not impossible, in mechanical signalling days. There are, for example, three possible routes off both Down roads through Everglades Junction station, to the Spur, Branch and Up Meadowside lines. The 'direct' routes have been determined as 'Loop to Spur' and 'Main to Branch', which means that diverging route indications are necessary for the other routes. But all the signalman needs to do is to set up the route, pull the relevant signal lever and the relays do the rest in advising the driver of his path. (Incidentally, at least three of the route indication lights must be proved alight before the signal will 'clear'). Exactly similar arrangements operate on signals covering the divergences to the Spur at Phillips Bridge Junction and into the Down Loop at Everglades. Some of these diverging routes are additionally protected by a system known as 'Approach Lock Release'. This is designed to ensure that a permanent speed restriction is adhered to by bringing a driver right up to a restrictive indication. Only when the engine hits the track circuit on the immediate approach to it will the signal change to its most unrestricted aspect.

To show how up to date GCR signalling practice is we need look no further than the signals leading up to the divergence of the Spur from the Up Main at Phillips Bridge Junction. There are, progressively, two automatic four-aspect signals followed by a controlled signal immediately in rear of the junction. When first installed the two 'autos' were designed to show, respectively, 'double-yellow' and 'single-yellow' aspects when the controlled one was cleared for the Spur. The problem for drivers in such circumstances was, of course, that under this system they had no means of knowing whether it actually was cleared in this manner or stood at 'danger'. This was a retrograde step from the arrangement in operation up to 1978 when the second auto was installed to break up this heavily-used section into two parts, for it replaced a 'splitting banner repeater' that showed the state of the controlled signal and so provided early warning. But the problem was solved by adopting the then-new BR method of signalling 'High-Speed Trains' up to a diversionary route: both autos were fitted in 1980 with flashing yellow aspects to operate when the Spur route is signalled.

Up until the mid-70s, a Train Register was kept in Hardwick Box to record movements in and out of the station and so monitor the number of trains run each working day. As traffic increased though it became too time-consuming to maintain properly and the function was covered for a time by a counter in the Everglades Junction relay room. Electrically operated, this was moved one number forward by each occupation of the track-circuit in advance of the Up line signal at the foot of Hardwick Bank. The information is now provided by the train describer.